Marryin'
Sam
Speaks
Out

Marryin' Sam Speaks Out

Arthur A. Rouner, Jr.

BAKER BOOK HOUSE
Grand Rapids, Michigan

Introduction

Marryin' Sam, as the Al Capp fans among the readers of the funnies will know, is a prominent citizen of the mythical town of Dogpatch in the back-woods "hollers" of Kentucky. It is down in the land of "Kickapoo joy juice," where every bad guy is a "varmint," and sexy, shapely Daisy Mae in her cut-off hot pants is forever chasing Mammy Yokum's handsome, muscled, backwoods boy, Li'l Abner. Marryin' Sam is the key figure of that community in giving dignity and legality to the budding relationships between men and women. For a fee, of course! And with the most minimal requirements. And certainly no marriage counseling.

Which is why I sometimes feel like Marryin' Sam. Not that the town I live in is a Dogpatch. Far from it. I live in one of America's typical suburbs where young families have come to raise their kids, and where for years there have been zillions of marriage-able young people.

And guess who does much of the marryin'? Yours truly. Like thirty or forty weddings a year. That's a lot of people getting "hitched" (as they say in Dogpatch!)

Naturally, you try to have some principles about it. You don't marry just anybody who comes along. You try to meet with them two or three times before the rehearsal and the wedding. You try to get them ready. To tell it like it is about marriage.

But sometimes there are so many, and they are so immature, that you become discouraged about the whole marriage business. How in the world are you going to keep people married? What can you do to get some of these young kids started right? And what with the local Christian Scientists with no ministers of their own who come to you to get married, and a bunch of other hangers-on, sometimes you wonder if you really do have any principles at all! Sometimes as you see some of your own earlier marriages breaking up, you wonder if you haven't become just a marriage broker, legalizing any old relationship that comes along. "Maybe I'm just a Marryin' Sam after all," you say.

But whether that's true or not, sometime the day comes when you say, 'I've got to speak out! Something's happening to marriage in America; and if it isn't any better than this among the Christians, think what it must be among those who have nothing in the way of faith! I'd better tell 'em what I know, and what I hope and dream for 'em right now while there's still time."

But, of course, maybe there isn't time. Maybe the kids in their late teens and early twenties getting married won't think that the country parson, with all his piety, is the person to advise them—especially about such worldly-wise things as sex and the other intimacies of married life.

I insist on seeing young couples at least twice, for an hour each time, before any wedding I perform. The vibrations I often get as they settle down in my study for the first session say something like, "Who does this jerk think he is, presuming to tell us the facts of life and love when he's nothing but a pious, ivory-towered minister? Why doesn't he just get on with it, set the date, make the arrangements, and be done with it?"

In fact, for a while, years ago, I used to fudge on sex and say, "Now, about the sex bit, why don't you see your family doctor?" But in the meantime, I've been convinced the family doctors haven't passed along much more than the biological facts of life, plus a little birth control information. So, drawing a deep breath, I've decided that—on the basis of having stayed married to one woman for twenty years, of being the father of five children, of having married and counseled over three hundred couples, and of having gone through divorces and affairs and most of the other inner struggles of married life with a host of more "mature" couples—I'd better give 'em the word myself: about the whole thing—sex as well as religion.

This book is a little of what I've learned about marriage. It's my concern as a Christian and as a minister for a generation of beautiful young people whom I love very much.

I write it because I have discovered dozens and scores of fine young people—many of whom have grown up in the life of the Christian church and in at least nominally Christian families—who haven't the foggiest idea what morality in marriage, much less Christian morality, might be. And in the meantime, the statistics are going against us. Divorce stands as a ready option to married couples, with one out of three couples throwing in the towel. Communal and even some other styles of relationship between men and women are being more openly and seriously tried. And, well, it just seemed a good time for Marryin' Sam to speak out!

If what he says makes sense to you, and helps

you think about what marriage is really like, and especially if it gives you a little running start on yours, then that makes me very happy.

It will make my secretary, Mrs. Lois Collings, happy too, because she typed the manuscript, and did it, as always, out of love—not only for me, but for all kids, like her young son, who may just read it. I give her my thanks, and give it also to those hundreds of young friends who have been honest enough to share with me their sometimes beautiful and sometimes heartbreaking experiences.

Here's to more and more of the beautiful kind!

Arthur A. Rouner, Jr.

The Colonial Church of Edina
Minneapolis, Minnesota

Contents

1

Does a New Generation Need a New Morality?

She was such a forlorn little girl sitting there in my study, all alone, facing such a great big problem. She must have looked pretty glamorous on a good many occasions; but on that day all the lipstick was gone, her mouth was held in a tight, thin line, and her face was pale and a little peaked.

Life was looking very different to her that day than it had three months before. The future didn't look quite as bright and carefree and promising as once it had . . . because she was going to have a baby. She had come to say to her minister, "What will I do?"

The little gal who came to see me that day is not just one little girl. She is many. She is thousands of girls who have been faced with the very unglamorous, little publicized, inevitable consequences of the social and sexual revolution going on in America and the world today.

Society hasn't much cared, in recent years, what the church thinks about sex and morality. But curiously, it is the church that reaps the problems after modern men have lived their new philosophy, and found, to their dismay, that it has brutal consequences! It is the church they want to marry them. It is the church they ask to help and counsel them. So the new morality of a new generation is the church's problem.

But, what is the problem? Not just little girls coming to confess they are pregnant and ask what should they do. That problem is as old as the history of man. It is the problem of what you have as a result when a society has subtly taught its kids, from a surprisingly early age, that sexual intercourse is something people do if they have a mind to, and that a lot of good guys and gals do it—both before marriage and outside of marriage—and that really, it's sort of okay. It's considered normal, and nobody is very serious about the old taboos.

In fact, what modern American society is specifically teaching is that hedonism, the seeking of pleasure, being happy—"doing your own thing"—is the way to go. It is not a new philosophy; indeed, it's the return of a very old philosophy. And it has had a powerful influence on several brief three or four year generations of kids.

It has been conveyed particularly through the news media and the entertainment industries. The billboards of America regularly treat us to the sight of flauntingly sexual women conveying some item for our purchase. Advertising has suggested to American young people that a woman is a sloe-eyed temptress in bikini panties, with huge breasts barely poured into a see-through brassiere, just waiting to inveigle some man between the sheets and pounce on him. If the Dodge Rebellion girl and the late night television model who looks over her shoulder and says, "Take it awl off!" aren't suggesting that, then I'm a dirty old man. The female is "used" by American advertising to sell, sell, sell; and the more seductive they can make her, the more they think she will sell.

The movie page—apparently without any principles or censoring on the newspaper's part—has become a peep-show of cartoons and photographs of women taking their clothes off, or in the act of embrace, with captions ranging from "naughty" to "perverse," suggesting that the scenes and language will reveal an intimacy in sexual relations that is too mature for kids, but quite okay for adults.

And of course, the films themselves go from scenes of brutal violence and strongly suggestive sex in GP rated pictures, through obvious scenes of sexual intercourse itself in R pictures, up to the naked multi-positioned sexual act displays in the newer and more frequent films that are X rated and indeed, beyond any rating!

Which is to say nothing of the stories, centerfold naked Bunny Girls, and articulated articles of a philosophy of pleasure purveyed in *Playboy* and the other magazines of its kind.

By the time you have Merv Griffin inviting a series of assorted singers, girls about town, and actresses on his late night show to talk brazenly about their sexual escapades outside of and in between marriages—egging them on with a bantering lustful gleam until one of them breaks into tears of shame at what she has been hearing—you have in America a corporate psyche pretty well saturated with a philosophy of sex as the self-serving and gratifying doing of "what comes natcherly." With no very widely heard voice in the land saying much of anything to counter it.

For all its tragic endings, films like "Joe" not only suggest that drugs are part of a deliciously full, temporary, and unobligating sexual experience (described by Joe as an orgy—hard G), but also that the young hippies who live that way are the really sensitive, human people of our time.

With the Willy-Boys, and a slew of other folk

heroes—often of minority races and espousing the great human justice causes—living sexual lives like that, what is a fourteen-year-old youngster to think about life and love other than exactly what is beamed at him in the blatant barrage of the magazines, movies, and media advertising that make up such a frighteningly large percentage of the daily input into the computer of his mind? Which doesn't even begin to speculate on the impact it is having on those thirty, forty, or fifty who are presumably well beyond those "impressionable" years!

Out of the assumptions of cultural life come the prevailing philosophies of any era. And the assumption of sexual availability and indulgence has undoubtedly produced a new philosophy of life in the mind of the generations of our time.

Most young people, even within the church, would hardly know what a "Christian view of morality"—sexual or otherwise—would be. Christian faith and philosophy, if you count church worship time, Bible reading, prayer, and discussion time, are allowed only minimal time in most people's minds when compared to the philosophy purveyed to us daily by radio, television, movies, magazines, and newspapers.

When you throw in the tolerance and the good-natured hesitation to be "judgmental" of the rest of us, you've got a conspiracy of forces that must look, to young people, like a plot in which the whole society is cooperating—even the church types.

In any case, what could be more natural than to begin to justify philosophically the acceptance of a life style which would obviously appear to be the kind of life most people are living? If you're fourteen, or sixteen, or twenty, and you're saddled with parents who seem to live and teach a different

14

philosophy, well, that just goes to show how really out of it they are!

Time after time, as kids have come to me, shocked to find that the girl is pregnant, they reveal that as their passions pulled them further along in sexual play, they did in fact, begin to justify it by saying, "Why isn't going to bed with each other okay as long as we really care about each other? Why shouldn't we go all the way in showing our love for each other as long as we're not hurting anyone else? After all, with the pill it's a whole new ball game!"

And of course it is. Sexual relations among collegians are quite clearly more open and more often than they were ten or twenty years ago. The dropping of parietal rules at Yale, for instance, means that girls spending weekends in the rooms of their boy friends (and vice versa with the advent of girl Yalies!) has become commonplace.

The philosophy is: "If it's there, why not take it? My personal life is my own private affair, and nobody else's business. I'm not hurting anyone else; and if I hurt myself, that's still my business."

That same view goes on to say, "After all, it's only right for every man to be free: free from racial oppression, free from unjust economic or social servitude, but also free from the pressure of the philosophy and ideas of others—especially parents, and suchlike."

What is especially devastating about it is that this philosophy has obviously justified the use of drugs as well as sex. Both have gotten mixed up in the right and good movement in our time toward easier and freer expression of love among friends, of a widespread commitment among the young to peace and racial justice, and of a desire for freedom and self-expression. These persons have justified in the use of drugs, at least, a break toward "freedom" that has been in reality a move toward bondage of the mind and will. Ultimately it has often led to a destruction of the self, ending in physical as well as spiritual and psychological death.

Indeed, because the young are so often "love-people," and "peace-people," and racial justice-people, and because the society against which they rebel is so often on the wrong side of these great human questions, the drug, sex, self sort of life has achieved a moral aura it does not deserve.

But it has produced a "new morality," aided not only by the Hugh Hefners of society, but even by theologians like Bishop John Robinson with his "New Morality," and Hamilton and Altizer with their "good news" that "God is dead."

The result has been for many people—particularly the young, but many of middleage—both a new philosophy and a new morality. That the young do not need a new morality is evident to the extent that the new morality they've found is based on a clearly false view of what a woman is, how she thinks, and what her psychology and purpose are.

The view that only doing one's own thing is all that counts is a direct contradiction of all that Jesus teaches about the call of the Christian man to deny himself and to lose his life for others, as a way of finding it.

Since the Christian philosophy of the value of people and the purpose of life has produced nobility and fulfillment in the lives of people for nearly two thousand years, it may have something inherent in it that makes it worth considering very seriously, in opposition to the new morality so glibly accepted and articulated by so many today.

Perhaps in the world of the pill, abortion, marijuana, LSD, rampant venereal disease, over-population, pollution, prejudice, and the bomb, it is important to see if there isn't a more "relevant" and maybe more eternal morality than the new morality, for the young and for us all.

2

The Heart Needs Christ As Well As Cupid

For the Christian, no morality without Christ is worth much as a working attitude and philosophy. Neat little ideas and lots of good advice are really beside the point without some real star to guide our existence, some solid rock for its foundation.

How you "feel" won't really do. Feeling spiteful one minute, or romantic the next, or carefree and cavalier afterward doesn't give you much to go on in the long haul of married life. "The heart," as they say, "is a lonely hunter." It is a will-o'-the-wisp. A wanderer, a stranger of many moods. And it can so easily get lost in the night. The love it once held so tenderly can evaporate so quickly.

I don't know how many fine, forty-year-old men have said to me about their wives: "I just don't love her any more." And women who've said: "I don't feel anything for George any more. My heart is dead."

And I believe them. I believe people can fall out of love. The cupid who shot his arrow through our heart when we were eighteen or twenty-two somehow isn't able to keep us hooked for a lifetime. Things change. We grow up, and grow older. Sometimes we become, in many ways, different people. In fact, a thousand things can happen to us that woo the heart away from its first loves, its highest ideals, and its most sacred promises.

So—there's got to be something more than the mood of the moment to go on. There's got to be something more than how I feel today—particularly if I'm wounded and mad at my wife or husband. There's got to be something that stands by itself, a measuring stick, a balancing wheel—to keep us straight and show us the way. We need something objective to give us a chance in marriage.

For one's heart needs something more than its own fickleness. It needs an anchor, a light, a guide. The Bible has this hope for our hearts: "That Christ may dwell in your hearts, by faith." That's what the lover's heart needs besides Cupid. He needs Christ.

Now don't tune out and say, "Forget it. This is just the same old pious stuff again that we always get from the churches. We know all about Christ, and He can't help in the problem of sex." I know that sex is a problem for Christians, just as much as it is for other people. I know they're not immune from the urges and desires that grow out of our sexual nature.

It's a temptation to think that the sexual urge and its consequent problems goes on regardless of faith or philosophy. It's easy to think that all we have here is the age-old urge of the sexes to unite—that we're fighting only the human bent for "doin' what comes natcherly!"

I think that's a big mistake. We take too low a view of man. He's more than an animal. He lives by dreams, he has ideals, he develops philosophies, and tries to live with them.

We all know that young people, in the course of their growing years, are drawn together, and tend to become more and more deeply involved with each other through the overwhelming power of love. We know about holding hands, and kissing good night, and necking in the park, and all that stuff. And we know how easily that turns into exploratory feeling of each other's bodies, and the increasing and almost desperate urge to "go all the way" by completing the act of love in sexual intercourse.

Very few adults today who fell in love during college days did not have a real struggle to fight off going all the way. And when we see a girl "in trouble," or a young couple in their struggle with sex, most of us are quite ready to sympathize and feel great compassion. We would admit with Moody: "There, but for the grace of God, go I!"

We've all struggled with the problem of sex. We're not lily-white on this. We know love is not a static relationship. It's always going one way or the other—either intensifying and progressing toward greater involvement, or diminishing and deteriorating as a relationship. If you're young and in love, you want to express that love for the other person more and more fully until you discover, perhaps to your horror, that there you are, just about to cross over that final line.

But what's the difference? Why do some go over the line—maybe with abandon—while others never do? I think it's because they have no great faith to keep them on the virginal side of the line. I think what's really true is that they have no Christ to give them the will to fight. They have no Christ to be their sword and shield and defender.

That's pretty tough, to be out there alone with "your cheatin' heart," and all your emotions. That's quite a battle to fight! And with too often no weapons to win it you can be a lost cause. Because then it's just you and your temptations. You and Satan out there—very often with Satan winning handily.

If indications of the high degree of sexual involvement of young people in high school—and even junior high school—have any validity, then a wise guess is that many people aren't fighting it at all.

Sin is a subtle and demonic thing. It fights against our wills. It attempts to brainwash us into doing the devil's thing, and not Jesus' thing. And often it succeeds. So often that it leaves us guilty and remorseful, fighting ourselves as well as the unseen enemy. Paul said it for all of us: "That which I would I do not; and that which I would not, that I do. O wretched man that I am, who shall deliver me from this body of death?"

Naturally, we are tempted to do things which we do not believe are right. That's what temptation is!

Most of us, however, don't continue indefinitely doing what we think is wrong. For then we can't live with ourselves. That's when our conscience accuses us, bugs us, until we do something about the dishonesty in our lives.

If, on the other hand, we continue in the inconsistencies of our lives, we may decide to accommodate our thinking to the new conditions and actions.

And this may be where the generation of this new day has the cards stacked against them. Because the so-called new morality of the 1960s wasn't invented and purveyed by the college kids, or the young swingers just a little older than they. They may, of course, want to have intercourse before marriage and want to justify it, and all that. They may even be down on marriage—thinking it's a useless institution used only as a device for legalizing and controlling the coupling together of people.

But if they knew of a better philosophy, "a better

22

idea'' as Ford says, and had a reason for wanting marriage to be a pure and sacred relationship, they would fight for that. They would prove capable of any struggle that any situation called for. The overriding reason would be a deeper commitment, a sense of their relationship to something or someone who means more than anything else in the world.

But the new morality is a philosophy of life; and tragically, it was developed by theologians. It has said—through interpreters like Bishop John Robinson of England—that what counts is two people's relationship. Like ''if we have a good relationship it's okay.'' If it's a bad relationship you don't ''do it'' because you don't love the girl enough, and if it's a good relationship you don't ''do it'' because you think too much of the girl and her honor to violate or compromise it.

And yet, while this could be interpreted as a good reason—real answers—for following the original Biblical teachings anyway about sex and adultery, it was soon backed up by other churchmen in other countries saying that yes, in some situations it's okay for two unmarried people to have intercourse. Like in Sweden where housing is scarce and it's economically hard for young people to get married. What young people have encountered is that even the church—or some parts of it—is telling them that a little experimentation is a good thing, that perhaps it will prevent some later grief.

Which, for a young person, is the only rationalization he or she needs! To hear the church saying, ''Fine, go along, give it a try! Who cares?'' is practically an open door for kids to rationalize their sexual indulgences, to cease fighting the good fight of faith.

And yet Jesus said: ''But I say unto you, if a man looks on a woman to lust after her, he has

committed adultery with her already in his heart."
It isn't that Christ is insensitive or unsympathetic.
He is strong and wise, and in the end, most loving.
And our task is to learn about loving. About real
loving.

And it is Jesus alone who really teaches that.
He teaches it in His life. He teaches it in His love
and respect for women, in His healthy view of sexual
intercourse as a beautiful, natural thing to do, in
marriage ("a man shall leave his father and mother,
and cleave unto his wife, and they shall be one
flesh").

Jesus is the one who has some ideals about marriage. He is the one who knows about love. He
is love. He died on the cross for love's sake—to
forgive us our sins of wrongly loving and of being
unloving. He comes with a whole different thrust
and purpose to life and love. He builds a very different kind of philosophy and point of view about love
and marriage.

If your philosophy of life becomes one that
believes intercourse with a girl before or outside
of marriage is okay, you will eventually begin to
live by that philosophy. You will practice what you
preach.

But if that's not what you want—if you have an
ideal, a dream, a hope for a married life someday
that is honest and unblemished by experimentation
with a lot of girls or a lot of guys, then the key
is to get Christ into your life: to make Him Lord
over your whole life; to put Him on the throne of
your heart and life. The job is to get Him on your
side. Enlist Him in your struggle for purity, and
honor, and character (not to speak of growing faith).

He is the one alone who can really help us with

24

the sexual fight. Nobody else will be there with us in the time of temptation—not our parents, or minister, or anybody. Certainly, in the back seat of a car, on a dark night, with someone you have flipped over, there won't be anyone to hold you back. Not even your best principles and ideals will be there. They may just as well have been put in cold storage.

But Someone will be there—out of love's purpose and for love's sake. And that is Christ. He is everywhere His friends ask Him to be. He promises to be with us.

So don't settle for just "love" in your sexual and later marriage relationships. Cupid, cute as he is, is not enough. The heart needs Christ as well as Cupid!

3

He Helps You Know If Your Love Is Real

One of the biggest questions I find young people have about the whole idea of marriage is: "How do I know if what I feel for this girl, or this guy, is real love? I mean, wow, we think we love each other. We certainly have fun together. And I guess we've gotten pretty intimate with each other—a lot of huggin', and kissin', and stuff like that. But how are you supposed to know for sure? What's the signal that says, 'This is the man or woman for me'? Is it something you just know, that makes you sure your love is the kind that can last forever?"

That's the question we all ask. People who are happily and long married probably couldn't say exactly what it was that made them sure of each other.

My experience is that it is at least something beyond feeling. There may well be more than one girl in the world who can give you butterflies in your solar plexus by her good looks, by the special smile she reserves for you, by that special tenderness in her eyes. There are many people in the world whom most of us could love. Many people who have a physical beauty, and a personal charm, and even some ideas and ideals that could really turn us on.

So the choice probably wouldn't be on physical and personal qualities alone. And I don't want to ignore the intangible quality of mystery—maybe mystique—that in the end decides us for one person or another.

My plea would be that, where other factors are more or less equal, there is one factor that makes more difference than you'd think. And that is faith. Whom does this person believe in? What is his or her life really committed to? As I ask couples, "What would you die for, if you were pressed to the limits? What cause, what passionate conviction, what person would you go all the way for? Would you, in fact, die for this person whom you think you love so much?"

This question is at least a start. Jesus says, "Greater love has no man than this, that a man lay down his life for his friend." That's pretty ultimate. A pretty deep relationship. A pretty final commitment.

So when you ask, "Is this real love?" you should mean, "Would I die for her? Do I love him enough so I'd even go through torture and death for him?"

While that's a little dramatic, suggesting something most of us will not have to do, it does move the whole question out from the shallows of physical attraction into the depths of the Spirit, and of the ultimate.

And who gets you there? Who draws you into those depths? Who says, "Come out here where it's over your head, and you've got to come through on something you've never been tested on before?" I believe Jesus does that. I don't know anyone else who puts life on the basis of fundamental commitments, of the nitty-gritty reality of eternal relationships. Isn't it possible, then, that it is only when you have a real Christ that you can have a real love?

The Bible says that God is love. It also says, "God was in Christ reconciling the world to himself." So Christ is where love is. Wherever love is, there, in some measure, if your heart is open and seeking, you can find Christ—or at least some glimmer, some reflection of Him.

I don't think any loving things get done in this world without the influence of Christ being in it in some way. He is God's great messenger of love in the world for all time. He is the reconciler, the bringer together of people, the smoother of ruffled feathers, and the giver of gentle tenderness.

Paul charges us, in our relationships with all people, to "be rooted and grounded in love." In other words, make love the foundation of our lives. And the way you get that foundation of love is through the gift of Christ, who is the source of love, the "port of entry" for love into the world.

If you want to have a marriage that will work, that will be strong and sure, with its foundation built on a rock and not on sand, you'd better build it on the deep love that Christ gives. Which is to say, build it on Christ Himself! On love for Him. On a shared love. On a common faith, on a common discipline, on a common caring about Him. That means praying and reading the Bible together, and serving others together. It's generally making Christ a part of your conversation, your thinking, your total life. Love each other in the Lord. See that you both are Christians. Worship God together. Go to Bible study together. Enter into the task of living with a Christian concern for other people. Be a team, in Christ. Be partners with Christ—together!

So much is healed when that kind of relationship is at the center of a marriage. So much is understood, so much forgiven. So much possibility and so many safeguards are built in for the future. Such a sure foundation is laid for that new life of two young people, because it is laid in Christ and His compassionate, self-sacrificing, healing kind of love.

America in the mid-mark of the twentieth century hasn't known an awful lot about love. It has fed itself on such a different and shallow understanding of what love is. Love, according to the American way of life, is a leering, voluptuous, sensual thing in which the blue-ribbon premium is put on the female body, and the sultriest look. America also sees love as being where the most daring baring of the bosom promises sexual bliss and happiness forever after!

But it's a deception. It's as false a picture of what love is as any that could be perpetrated on a generation of young people. Completely unreal. Because if that's what you're looking forward to, you will be bitterly disappointed when you finally are into marriage, and are living with the girl of your dreams. Because you will discover that she isn't a sex-pot, but rather a person. And she has her ups and downs, and good days and bad days, just as you do; and she has a lot of things that are important to her besides the sexual act. In the midst of real married life, you will find that there are many other things in love just as important to both of you than just bare sex.

Which is not to say that sex is out, or that the church is against it, and thinks sex is sinful and dirty. Far from it! Jesus Christ and the Christian faith have never said sex is a bad thing. Generations of misguided Christians (and too many of them parents) have thought it was a semi-bad thing and were ashamed even to talk about it. But the New Testament doesn't say that. Although neither Jesus nor

Paul chose the life of marriage for themselves, they both commended it. Sex they saw as something good. A man and his wife, Jesus said, "shall become one flesh." And there is every indication that they saw sex as good for more than just the procreation of children. The churches who have limited sexual activity to the begetting of children, and birth control therefore as unnatural and un-Christian, have seriously misunderstood the whole spirit of Jesus and His commending of love as a way of life. Because the sexual act is the fulfillment of one person's love for another. It says, "I love you all the way! I give you everything I have, and all that I am. I expose myself to you and enter into your life and your body! Love you? I am you!"

Intercourse is a way of loving! And the loving comes first, and is primary. Children conceived out of that act of love are a happy by-product, and surely part of the purpose of life. But the first purpose is love—a love that begins with the glance of the eye and the touch of the hand and culminates in the beautiful joining of the two bodies together. It is a good and holy thing.

The deepest meaning of sexual intercourse is in commitment. It is good and beautiful because it is the culmination of a promise—a public promise made in the eyes of all the world, and of God to love each other, to care for each other, and to encourage each other until death parts them.

So love is a promise. Love is pledging yourself to someone else, and you're not doing that when you enter into a sexual compact with someone before marriage or outside of marriage. Because it is in marriage that before the world, and before your friends and family you promise your life to the one you love.

31

That means you promise not just the kissing, loving, sexual times, but also the working times, the playing times, the child-raising times, the serving your fellow man and the serving God times. Real friendship is that which could demand even your life. Your husband or wife is meant to be your greatest friend. It is a whole life you promise to this person, not just the occasional promiscuous times of sexual urge which the world of Tom Jones, Elizabeth Taylor, James Bond, and Madison Avenue would have you think it is!

Sex is a part of a whole life you will have with someone you love. Wait for it. Prepare for it. Keep your philosophy straight and your faith right. And keep Christ at the heart of it. Then you will have something to bring to it: a real love, a love you are sure of, that comes to you through Christ. Your marriage will be "rooted and grounded in love."

4

Living Together in the Real World

Not long ago I heard a beautiful story about a young couple I knew. The boy had been a student of mine, years ago, in ninth grade confirmation. He's a big handsome guy, and had married a tall, beautiful girl; and they were going to college together out West.

I've always prayed about all of my young church kids, that the church thing wouldn't be just a formality; but that somewhere along the way they'd truly "get the Spirit." That they'd come to know Jesus in a vital way and become excited and exciting Christians.

The good news I heard about this boy and girl was that during their last year of college they'd had a tremendous experience of conversion, and had received Jesus into their lives, and had suddenly discovered that He was the greatest thing going. They were reading the Bible, going to meetings, praying together, and even getting themselves trained so that they could tell others about their Lord. I was thrilled for them, and excited at what had happened in their lives.

It was only later that I learned the full meaning of it. This young couple had had their experience of the person of Christ at a point in their young lives, and their early marriage, when the girl was in a hospital psychiatric ward in the midst of an emotional breakdown, the boy was despairing of their whole relationship, and their marriage was just about over.

Two beautiful kids from upper middle-class educated families of economic and social stability. Both families members of and more or less active in churches. On the surface it should never have happened.

But what had happened was almost routine. Far from home, wanting to be "free," and rationalizing their behavior as shedding the constricting limits of their traditional upbringing, they had begun using drugs, particularly marijuana, and had begun to swing with the ski set—doing all the "*apres*-ski" things you can do. They had temporarily dropped out of college to "find themselves," and had finally come to the point where they were so confused, and guilty, and resentful of each other that they knew they couldn't continue living with themselves or with each other.

They were horrified at the shock and shame that the breaking up of their marriage would bring to their parents and to them, and were very nearly unstrung by what they had done to themselves. Until one night, in the home of a friend, the boy heard a message of resurrection faith that was so sure, and fit so beautifully the need of his almost shattered life, that he knew its truth was for him. Evidently he ran immediately to that hospital floor, and broke in on his young wife with the news he had found. She, bless her heart, wanted to receive Christ in a church building, so went to find one and there invited Christ into her heart. And they have been new people. And their marriage is a new marriage.

They learned the hard way what it means, literally, to be saved. Their own lives had been saved. Their marriage had been saved. But one out of every three marriages in America is not saved. I wonder why. I wonder if it is because they, too, try to live a life that is unreal—a life that is pleasure-seeking and essentially purposeless, and in the end destructive.

So the problem for all of us who try to live a married life in the second half of the twentieth century in America is how to live together in the real world. Not in some false world of unreal expectation. Not in some improbable world of no problems, no responsibilities, no disappointments, and no failures, but in the real world of very human people who are incorrigibly selfish. They are people who love themselves more than anyone else, who are frighteningly adept in their ability to do cruel things to each other, and who are somehow very prone to doing a whole lot of stupid and unworthy things in life—things of which they are often ashamed afterward.

That's the world where marriage is really at. That's the scene in which you've got to make it with another person: not the rose-colored glasses scene of the college romance, the giggling showers, the roomsful of glittering wedding presents, the rehearsal dinner, the candle-lit wedding, and the country club reception.

The marriage scene is when it's you two, alone at last, facing each other, and now having to live together. It's brushing your teeth together, looking at each other across the breakfast table, seeing the baggy eyes or the hair in curlers, going off to work or to classes. It's coming home at the end of the day and helping out, and giving pleasure, and trying not to be a bore—reading, talking, learning, growing, loving for the other person, come what may, and trying to be most helpful and fun to live with.

What you discover is that it's so easy to be a grouch—to pout and stamp your foot, and want things your way. It's not to try to be a couple together, but to go too far with Kahlil Gibran in being "close but not too close, for the pillars of the temple stand apart . . ." etc., etc., and like my young married friends in college, just doing your own thing. Maybe doing it so completely that after awhile, you no longer have a marriage. You've lost it in the self-thing, the getting-your-own-way thing. And you end up a hurt, angry person, going through a divorce battle with somebody you once dearly loved, fighting—of all things—over who's going to get the money and who gets the kids. And by that time you're a wounded woman, or a bitter man. But that never was what marriage was about. You never got the point. You never really tried it. You never gave it an honest chance.

To be ready to live—live in the real world, not the false world—I think you've got to have something God gives. You've got to have the humility and openness that is able to grow into maturity. And by maturity I mean the ability to laugh a little (especially at yourself), and to be wise enough to know that today's disaster will not always hang around, just as today's triumph may one day turn into defeat. It's the ability to have that John Kennedy gift of "grace"—"courage under pressure." It's the knowledge that life is an on-going stream, that it is one war consisting of many battles, and that sometimes the better part of valor is to take a defeat today in order to live to fight again tomorrow.

Maturity somehow has to include hope: that quality in the human spirit that doesn't give up, that believes in the future, that feels it is worthwhile to go on. And hope is built on faith. For, as the Book of Hebrews defines it: "Faith is the substance of things hoped for, the evidence of things not seen." All of which is a lot like the apostle Paul's wish that we may know "what is the breadth, and length, and depth, and height" of the love of Christ, "which passes knowledge."

You just can't get away from the love of Christ, from the loving tolerance and kindness and understanding of the one man in all of human history who really knew what it was all about: who knew how people hurt each other, and get off on the wrong foot, and pull boo-boos, and so easily and unwittingly destroy themselves—and often others. His love overcomes even that! His love beats all the "knowledge," of the world.

Lots of people know many things but still manage to mess up their own lives and those of others. I know top psychiatrists whose daily business is helping other people sort themselves out. That involves educating them in the art of self-knowledge and the ability to live with others. It means helping these side-tracked individuals who cannot see the forest for the trees in their own lives when they find themselves in love with their office nurse, or secretary, or somebody else half their age, making absolute fools of themselves in the eyes of their grown-up families and professional colleagues as they set out in all seriousness to break up their homes to marry the passing sweetheart of their middle-aged adolescence.

Smart? Oh, yes. Knowledgeable about humankind and its fanciful foibles? Oh, yes. But in their own situation, in their own need, knowledge does not save them. But Paul, and Jesus, and all those other faithful guys of yore, insist that the love of Christ will! It "passes knowledge." It's better than knowledge because it has power to do what knowledge cannot do.

It has power, for instance, to forgive. It has power to lead a young husband to step over his wounded pride and actually say, "Honey, it was stupid of me to say that, and I'm sorry. Will you forgive me?" And in most cases that's all that's needed.

Life is so trial and error that you'll never be always right. And if you know that, then you'd jolly well better get in touch with someone who is right and who knows what right and truth are—indeed, who is truth. And truth, marriageable young friends, is Jesus. "I am the way, the truth, and the life," He said.

In spite of the supersentimentality with which the church has surrounded Him at times, Jesus is the one who knows about life. Who's been around. Who knows where it's at and who can show us how to live, especially in marriage. It's because He knows what the purpose of life, and love, and marriage really is.

Lots of people in our society try all sorts of things over the years, and think that each of them is really life. Some become sexually involved with someone who is not their marriage partner. Some drink too much at cocktail parties. Some do things in their business transactions which are not quite honest. Some sit glued before television and never read a book. Some never have time for their kids. Some are consumed with ambition and driving for success. And many think that Jesus Christ is for old women and little children.

But they all grow old. And one day, if they are at all thoughtful, they look back over their lives and wonder about its purpose. They may even ask themselves secretly: "What was it all about?" And often they see to their dismay that life has been slipping away, and that they are only now beginning to see that what they had lived wasn't really "life" at all. They finally see their idea of "really livin' " as wide of the mark.

Living a real life of marriage means you've got to have a purpose. You've got to have a great love in your life. Even greater than your own love. A power greater than your own needs to work in your mind and heart. As the first James Dean said, you have "to be dedicated."

There is only one person I know of who can give that dedication. It is only Christ who can actually do this for people. And giving your hearts to Him, as a married couple, is one way that you will be set free to be yourself, to love someone else, and to live with that person through fifty years or more, in joy and in love.

That's real life. A great life to have together!

5

Knowing the Difference Between a Man and a Woman

"Dearly Beloved, we are gathered here in the presence of God to join together this man and this woman in holy matrimony; which is instituted of God, regulated by His commandments, blessed by our Lord Jesus Christ, and to be held in honor among all men . . . . Into this holy estate these two persons present come now to be joined."

I have said these words at least three hundred times. But the scene has always been the same. The expectant hush of a church in late afternoon or early evening, the almost awe-filled faces of a host of friends and family, and directly before me a slightly nervous young man and an almost always radiant and beautiful young woman.

It is their wedding day, and they have come to give their lives to one another, to share one life, one high and hopeful destiny. And I have been the privileged one given the grace to make them man and wife.

I have loved and rejoiced with them all, and many of them are still my special friends. But sometimes I wonder what it all means to those I marry. Sometimes I wonder how they've prepared for that great day and that new life; and even more I wonder not only what their expectations are, but how much they know. About life and marriage, yes; but particularly about each other.

Not that I hope they've already done the sexual thing. My hope is quite the opposite of that. Too often I find that hardly with a by-your-leave of the morality in which they were reared, they have gone to bed with each other apparently without an after-qualm—except when that act of intercourse, to their surprise and chagrin, has conceived a baby!

Yet, even with these worldly-wise sophisticates who would seem to know so much about the facts of life and love, I find myself wondering how much they really know about the subtleties of sex in marriage.

At the point at which I suggest the subject of sex for our discussion, I note with amusement the faint flicker of condescension in their smiles. "Don't tell me this preacher is going to try to tell us about sex! Surely we're not going to have to sit through this, are we?"

I guess it's easy for all of us to think we know it all. And it's a great temptation to view people—maybe especially preachers—as stereotypes. Anyway, I try to put them at their ease by laughingly listing my qualifications as a husband of twenty years, as a father of five, and as a marrier of many.

The point I try to make is that there's a difference between a man and a woman. First reaction: what could be more obvious? The outer sexual differences are obvious; but they are symbolic of inner psychical differences that are not.

Look at humankind: men really are very different from women. And God wanted it that way. Jesus said: "Have ye not read that he which made them at the beginning, made them male and female?" God didn't want man to be lonely on the earth, so He

42

said, "I will make an help-meet for him." And after making woman out of man's rib He has Adam say: "This is now bone of my bone, and flesh of my flesh: she shall be called woman, because she was taken out of man . . . ." And the last word of the story is "And they were both naked, the man and his wife, and were not ashamed."

Think of it! Those wonderful days before clothes: when what you wore or didn't wear couldn't make you one bit more glamorous than the next girl, and when no Arrow shirt or London suit could tell the world you were rich or poor. You were just plain "you."

But, of course problems came, even back there in the Garden of Eden. For envy and pride and sin came; and sin brought shame and the awareness of nakedness, and cowering behind bushes, as you well remember. And that's how clothes came.

But the point nevertheless remains: God made us different, and "Vive la différence!" He wanted man to be man, and woman to be woman. He wanted us to be attracted to each other. He liked beautiful bodies, and lovely hair, and fetching smiles, and bewitching eyes. He liked men to be strong, with features clean, and noble brows. He made us that way. He labored over man and woman. He fashioned the eye and the hand, and the lip and the ear, the leg and the arm. We are His artistry—the work of His hand, His creation. "And God looked at everything that he had made," the Bible says, "and behold, it was very good."

Nothing wrong with sex—not from God's point of view, and not from the church's either. God made it, and it's good. Be beautiful, He's saying, put your hair up, wear fetching clothes, walk with a clean and graceful step. As for us men, there's not much we can do but hold our tummies in, keep the soup off our shirts, and polish our shoes.

Sex is good, made for us by a good God; yet nothing in all the world palls faster when it is mistreated. Nothing loses its glamor, rouses resentment, and causes grief in the heart when it is misused more quickly than does sex. For years I have sat in my study and listened to the sorrows sex has brought to the unmarried as well as to the married. And some of those sorrows had their source in a failure at the beginning of marriage to know the difference between a man and a woman.

Women, for one thing, are cyclical. Men are constant. Physically, a girl's menstrual pattern suggests that her nature is cyclical. But her spirit, too, is cyclical. Very affectionate one day, she is distant and cold another. She is a person of moods, and they are part of her charm. Warm and cuddly one moment, wild and free the next. Hair up, hair down; mood giggling, mood serious. A guy never knows what to expect. And he loves her for that very variety.

But often he doesn't bargain for the reflection of that infinite variety in his bride's sexual pattern, too. American advertising, and perhaps even his courtship, has suggested that sex with his beautiful young wife who loves him will be passionate and consuming, all night, every night. Dreamer! It's never so. Because she's a person. And she is an inward person who sometimes just wants to be alone.

But he is shattered. Again and again his ego is crushed, for he feels he's been rejected. "How come?" he asks. "You were never that way before we were married!" Well, hopefully, they weren't going to bed before they were married. And intimacy has exposed depths that neither guy nor gal were prepared for.

Which doesn't mean they can't be lived with. But only with great sensitivity and compassion will they be lived with. The young man feels personally rejected, unloved; while, in fact, a withdrawal of love couldn't be further from the mind of the young bride. She's always instinctively known these things about herself; but she never realized just how this would affect another person's life, especially that of the man of her dreams. He not only feels hurt and wounded, but wonders if his wife is frigid—a cold, unresponsive woman whose courting tenderness and affection completely misled him!

She, on the other hand, is now aghast to discover that this young man, with whom she fell in love partly at least "because he is so stable, so solid and sensible; I feel so secure with him . . ." is just as "stable," just as "solid," just as much like clockwork in his sexual attentions as he is in his many other virtues.

And she hadn't counted on that! "Why, he's always ready for sex," she protests. "At the drop of a hat (or a slip) he's ready to jump into bed with me. I'm beginning to think he's a sexual maniac, that he's oversexed and just interested in my body!"

Can't you hear her saying: "You beast, when are you going to care about *me* and not my body?" She didn't reckon on this wonderful young man's "dependability" extending all the way into his sexual life.

The accusations flung back and forth need only to be imagined. And the hurts and wounds inflicted are many. Because they didn't understand the essential, natural difference between a man and a woman.

The key is to remember that in none of these differences is love challenged or questioned. The girl does not hold back from intercourse with her young husband because she doesn't love him, but because she is made differently from him. She has different needs.

Nor is the pressing sexual interest of this young man a sign that he is all lust, with no real love in his heart. It is that he is different. They each, by nature, express their love in a different way.

For a woman, totality is what she seeks: affection and kindness and attentions that span a whole day and create an atmostphere of love that leads logically and inevitably to the bedroom. She's a mood person. And failures of character, like forgetting to take out the garbage, are remembered by her and harbored up against her lover.

To him these little acts of kindness, while important and virtuous, have no relation to his love for his wife and their sexual expression of that love. He has been away all day, arriving home late at night, just longing to be taken into the arms of his beloved and sheltered at last from the cruelties of the world out there. But her retort may come, with eyes flashing, "Forget it, Buster! You never kissed me good-bye this morning, or emptied the trash!"

In the same vein, he may complain of his wife's lack of attentions only to have her hit back with, "Well, I baked you a pie, didn't I? Didn't that tell you I loved you?" And truthfully, it hadn't. Not in the sexual way—the way in which he longs for signs of love.

Misunderstanding. Such great potential hurt. Because they didn't know the difference, in the beginning.

But with love, and most of all, with gentle faith

and patient dealing with each other in great forgiveness, they can know the differences, and work within them, and be glad for every one of them!

6

Where Did Marriage Come From?

One of the most beautiful ideas I know about marriage is that it was made in heaven. That it was God's plan that men and women should live this way together. And that every time a boy and girl fall deeply in love, and dream of living, and loving, and laboring together through life, God has something to do with it.

To me that's a beautiful, beautiful thing: that falling in love with the right girl or guy isn't just luck or chance. But that just as the flowers grow, and the seasons come, and day follows night, and the whole natural world is full of relationships according to the plan of God—so the most beautiful relationship of all between those creatures of His whom God loved most should also be part of God's plan for them.

Which does not deny the sorrows of life—where a young woman's life of love is frustrated again and again and her existence becomes a lonely one of "old" maidenhood. Nor does it deny the terrible disappointments so many people have in marriage, and the scene it becomes of cruelty and unkindness and just awful hurt. Those are the sad exceptions, the denials, and frustrations, and even defiance of God's plan of love for His children.

But if it's true that "if God so clothes the grass of the field which today is, and tomorrow is cast into the oven, will he not much more clothe you, Oh ye of little faith," isn't it clear that God cares even more for His human children than for the earth which He has so beautifully made? And if He has a plan for the earth and its seasons, and the plants and the animals, doesn't He also have a plan for us and our love? After all, what is more important to every one of us than our relation of love to someone dear to us—except our love for Christ Himself?

Why not, then, a plan, a special person, one man or woman in all the earth who was made for us and we for him or her? Is that so fantastic? So naive?

Maybe the very reason why some love relationships have so much pain, and some marriages so much grief, is because those people never did seek, in Christ's spirit and love, the person God meant for them. Maybe it's because in so many marriages lust was the motivation, and marriage was made only out of the unspoken longing of two people to have each other's bodies. Maybe some of us ask for trouble in our marriages because we insist on thinking our love for another human being has nothing to do with God. Maybe lots of people married each other for the wrong reasons, and are miserable because they did not, in faith as well as love, wait till they found "the one" who was right in God's eyes.

I'm a little ashamed of myself that half-facetiously I point out to the bridal couple, at the wedding rehearsal, the phrase in the opening prayer of the marriage service that says, "As Thou hast brought them together in Thy providence." I'm embarrassed because I laugh about it and offer it to them simply as an idea which they can accept or not. I believe now I should offer it much more seriously as an essential ingredient of every Christian marriage.

Because, if these two people getting married did not find themselves according to "God's providence," they're in for trouble. They'd better give up right now their pseudosophistication that is offended or embarrassed to think that God had something to do with this choice that they rather proudly thought was all their own.

The evidence that's in suggests that marriage, as a publicly initiated and recognized relationship between a man and woman, is an institution that came first out of man's relationship with God, and therefore out of his faith, rather than out of purely legal relationships performed and recognized in a secular, civil way.

According to the Genesis account, it was God who not only created both man and woman, but it was He who gave woman to man to be his wife. God, not secular courts and kings, made marriage. In primitive relationships, according to history and anthropology, it was a matter of mating and of animal instinct—as it is with lesser animals today.

But marriage, as a way of life of two people committed to each other, is God's institution. As the Christian wedding service says it, marriage is "instituted of God, regulated by His commandments, and to be held in honor among all men." And it was "for this cause," Jesus said, that "a man shall leave his father and mother and cleave unto his wife."

Our society is very vague about this. Marriageable young people know that the state is involved in the marriage business—like you need a license from the county courthouse, and sometimes a blood test, just to make it all legal. But the ideal is still a churchy sort of thing, with many of them feeling that somehow they'd like to have their wedding performed in a church. Why? Well, they really don't know. "It seems a little more sacred that way, I guess." Or, "Well, I just always thought I'd like to be married in a church."

Had they thought of a church wedding as a distinctive act of faith, implying that bride and groom believed in God, and were Christians, and were specifically bringing God in on their marriage? No, they certainly hadn't.

The church wedding has become part of the furniture. It's one of those things you do, but not something you plan for and seek out as a specific testimony to the personal faith of the couple. Only in rare and beautiful instances is it really that, I'm afraid.

Of course, when they come to the church to arrange for the wedding, we very quickly try to engage the kids in a discussion of the meaning of marriage. We emphasize its basis in faith, and the beauty and power that are added to both the wedding service and married life when they are begun as an act of faith, as a sacred moment, in the church.

That at least says, "This hour is God's, and we want it to be!" And my experience is that most couples, after they've talked about it awhile, do want their marriage to succeed and do want God to be part of it. In fact, it's rather an exciting idea to them when they discover that God is really what marriage is all about! That He's the one who really knows about love. He's the one from whom the loving ingredients of forgiveness and tenderness and understanding come.

They're not against it. It's just that, tragically, the God idea is so new to them. They've rebelled against the church and its formalisms, and didn't realize that, to be quite consistent, they should throw out the traditional formalism of the marriage service too; and that maybe they're not so against formality, and tradition, and heritage as they thought.

They're not sure about the future, and about being church people themselves. But they're open, and they want to make at least a beginning of their life together with God. My delight is to find how many of them, once they're onto the God thing, are eager to do something with it, to make the wedding service distinctly personal, and very much a testimony of the faith and concern they do have.

They want their wedding to be meaningful. They want it to remind the guests of God. It has made for this minister some tender and strangely moving marriage services in the last few years.

It's so easy to make a wedding just one big social bash. A time for the mother of the bride to come cruising in as the Great White Arranger, to have the moment in the sun she's been waiting for ever since her daughter was born. So easy to lay on lavish trimmings, with the makings of a private palm forest being brought over from the florists, and so to set the scene that all the guests will be duly impressed. Bring out the bridesmaids in the latest fashion and make a beautiful white doll of the bride—all this as a splendiferous and sentimental prelude to the reception which will follow at the country club, and hopefully be marked as a highlight of the social scene.

These are the weddings—(fewer and fewer I am grateful to say) where the wedding party have just come from drinks when they arrive for the rehearsal. It's where the bridesmaids come loud and thoughtless on the wedding day to dress at the church, leaving cigarette stubs as well as coat hangers, plastic bags, pins, and whatnot strewn over what must be third grade Sunday school classrooms the next day. It's where ushers thoughtlessly stand smoking in the back of the church ten minutes before the service. It's where the bride has been tranquilized up to here in order to—as her mother says—get through her wedding day. Most assuredly an exercise in sacrilege from the viewpoint of the dismayed cleric.

It is usually these weddings, too, where the big emphasis of the reception is the chance for free drinks, and where the father of the bride ends up as the most sodden one of all.

That is a tragic enactment for any wedding, even those in the most sophisticated and social families, and plainly does not need to be. More and more of today's young people sincerely want their marriage service to say something—not only to them but also to the families and friends who are there. In fact, they are eager to make a "testimony"—at least of sincerity and meaning and hope, and often of real and growing faith as well.

After all, they could go to a local justice of the peace and have their wedding done very quickly, very cheaply, and with a minimum of fancy fanfare and feeling. Particularly after their first session or two in my study, where the claims of faith and their necessary commitment to an open pilgrimage with Christ are rather heavily laid to them, they could very quickly decide to go the judge, or mayor, or captain of the ship route!

But instead, here they come to the church, in spite of all. Somehow, when all is said and done, they do believe that "love is eternal"; and they honestly do want their wedding day to be a sacred and beautiful memory.

And doesn't that fit in with a marriage "made in heaven"? If this beautiful girl, or that handsome guy, is that one person in all the earth who, in the mind of God, has always been waiting just for me since the beginning of time, well then, we want our wedding day to be the most beautiful day in our lives.

And I think on that day, most young couples would like to believe that after life here is done, there will be in that afterland which only God knows, and where love dwells eternally, a great reunion not only with God Himself, but also with the dear companion of the days of our married life here.

Isn't that why Elizabeth Barrett could write to her Robert:

I love thee with the breath,
Smiles, tears, of all my life!—and, if God choose,
I shall but love thee better after death.

Isn't that worth waiting for—fifty years, or even only five years, of pure joy and honest love with someone God meant you to have, rather than one wild, turbulent, ecstatic night with someone you do not truly love. The wrong kind of relationship, whether the wrong kind of marriage or the sexual experiences of a relationship that never dared to be marriage, can only be ashes in the mouth compared to the sweet and beautiful thing that love—and particularly God's love—in marriage brings.

Sometimes those things that are worth waiting for, and preparing for, and giving up something for, are the best in life. Sometimes even the God things —the things that used to look churchy, and pious, and holier-than-thou—are ultimately the most personally satisfying in the end. I would declare this to be true in every marriage when young people haven't been ashamed to take it from God as His special and beautiful gift to them.

7

Being One with Another, Yet True to Yourself

If one thing is true in all the world it's that everyone wants to be loved. You can make it a rule: there isn't anybody, anywhere, who doesn't want to be loved. The most bitter people-haters ever, have chosen to be that way because they feel ugly and unloved.

That means that the world can be won by love. Other minds can be changed, angry attitudes can be overcome, perverse personalities can be transformed. Love can do all that.

There's a little bit of God in all love. Maybe it's that in love that reaches out in such openness and gentleness and takes the other person by surprise, and breaks down his defenses, and reconciles him. So, when you're dealing with love, you're dealing with the most potent force the world knows.

It is the one most vital force affecting all our lives. You need to be loved as a tiny baby if you're to have half a chance in the world. Mental disorder very often dooms the young unloved. And the worst battle of the soul for the growing army of the aged is the feeling of being rejected and unloved. And in middle life, at the height of his powers, the man who says he needs no one—nothing but his work—is fooling himself. He is striving for someone's love—the love of wife, or children, or secretary, or maybe the world "out there."

And the way love is fulfilled, the way it is most exciting and rewarding—like a courtship, like having your tummy go flip-flop when you even see that special girl or guy—is when it is shared. When each one gives something to the other. And all you really have to give, in love, is yourself: your heart, your dreams, your deep feelings, your song, your spirit, into someone else's keeping.

He gives to you, and you give to him. If only one person is giving then it is idolatry, and not love. It is hero worship or goddess worship, but it's not love. Nothing is coming back, nothing is being shared.

Of course, if you do share, you're taking an awful risk. Because true love doesn't give away something cheap, or dispensable. True love gives away itself. It's inner things, secret things. It's your innermost being that you give to your lover, and the unwritten plea that goes with it is "Please don't trample on me. Don't ridicule me. I've no defense, no hidden retreat left if you don't take me, and accept me, and love me back!"

Oh, it's precious! Love given is indeed precious. It must be held with gentle hands, and cherished, and defended. It's a little like the beautiful rendering in *The Living New Testament* of Paul's words to the Corinthians: "If you love someone you will be loyal to him no matter what the cost. You will always believe in him, always expect the best of him, and always stand your ground in defending him" (I Cor. 13:7).

Love is that kind of sharing, of taking the other's part, of identifying of yourself with the other. And if you don't give yourself away into the other's keeping and receive that other into your own keeping—well, it isn't really love!

Jesus gave this as the acid test of love: "Greater love has no man than this, that a man lay down his life for his friend." Which is what He did, finally, for all of us. He gave Himself, completely. And if He hadn't gone all the way, if He had stopped somewhere short of death itself, we would know that He loved Himself more than us. There would then be no redemption, no salvation.

Giving your life away, not only to the other person, but for the other person (which is very much the same thing) is the final test, then, of our love too. Most of us in this life are not pressed to that extremity. We dream of living a lifetime together with our loved one, and reaching old age rich in shared years and shared memories. But true love believes that it is always ready to go that far for the other, and lives in the assumption that if ever put to that ultimate test for the loved one, it would not fail.

And yet, it is this giving, this sharing, this entering into the life of the other one that scares us most about getting married. And young love, whether for "women's lib" or just plain individuals' "lib," makes much of holding something back, of "being myself," or "refusing to lose my own identity in my husband's, or my wife's identity." And the "pillars of the temple," standing apart, are quoted, and Gibran's man and woman also standing apart.

Imagine! "Eat bread together, but not from the same loaf!" Why not from the same loaf? That's the whole significance of Christian communion, as in the Lord's Supper the common, single loaf is broken and shared, just as Jesus' body was broken for the world and shared with the world.

The significance of married love is that two lives become one life. They become one common enterprise, one shared experience, one single adventure. Anything that touches one cannot help touching the other. No victory nor defeat can come into the life of one without also coming into the life of the other.

That's what it's about. "No man is an island entire to itself. Each man's death diminishes me." That's how John Donne expressed it in all human relationships. Ruth said, in her beautiful words of commitment to one she loved: "Whither thou goest I will go, and where thou lodgest, I will lodge; where thou diest, I will die; thy people shall be my people, and thy God my God." Or, as a great modern medical missionary, Jim Turpin, says: "Love you? I am you!"

In marriage it is this that is symbolized by the act of sexual intercourse. Here the yearnings of the heart and of the body for that complete physical sharing that draws two people together, is fulfilled. The two lives become the one new life—even to the point of literally conceiving new life! For Jesus said: "And they twain shall be one flesh."

It is God's will and purpose that a man and woman in love should become one life—not just in spirit or mind, but even in body: "one flesh," as the Bible says. There once was a day when, in order to keep it pure and holy, Protestant theology (and Catholic theology too, before it) made the sexual act something shameful, and dirty, and done in darkness. Something only to whisper about. Generations of young people grew up thinking it was bad, and were caught in an agony of anxiety, and frustration, and fear over it.

But, it is not an enemy. It is not shameful, or dirty, or bad. It is beautiful! It is the fulfillment of life when it is practiced with love, in marriage. And only in marriage, because only then can it fulfill the total commitment of one life to another which the physical entering into another person is meant to symbolize. In marriage, sexual intercourse becomes the complete giving of oneself to another in love. Not only have you said it—you've done it. Intercourse is the most powerful nonverbal expression that there is. It's a gift you give. A beautiful, sharing gift.

Indeed, as already suggested, it is so basic a gift of sharing in the human experience, that it is the giving of the gift of life itself. The giving not only of your life to your beloved, but also a new life to her, or him. It's the giving of a child—a new life to the world.

Not that giving birth to children is the only purpose of sex. Rather, it is a beautiful and happy by-product of the sexual act. It's a special mystery, a miracle, that God lets us share in, as we become instruments in His purpose. And my experience is that conceiving and giving birth to a child is often the first great inexplicable miracle that happens in the lives of two young people. It is this, often more than anything else, that humbles their youthful pride, and sends them to their knees, and lifts up their eyes to behold, in awe and majesty, the hand and the heart of God.

And if conceiving children in sexual intercourse puts us, from time to time, directly in the plan of God's purpose for life, then it is logical to think that He intends a man and woman to be living with each other in a relation of such commitment, and permanence, that they can be the instruments for bringing these little human beings into the world, preparing them to make their contribution of promise and destiny in the world. And what can that commitment be, other than marriage? What can it be but two people committing their resources, their personalities, their common caring to each other for the long future?

And is that so bad? Is that the permanent loss of individuality? In giving himself to another person in marriage does the partner lose himself in that other one? Has he given something away that can never be taken back, or that is somehow lost forever?

Not as God would have it! In His plan it is an adding to the other person, not a taking away. Each one receives a new dimension, a new security, and therefore a new joy and freedom. Because he is loved! The lifelong struggle of every human soul to be loved has found fulfillment, has achieved its raison d'être. And that haunting fear of never being loved is overcome by love's gift, so that the personality now is more fulfilled, and more free to fully and truly be himself. Youthful worries can be put aside, as in the strength and sunshine of another's love, the lover can go out and share himself gladly with the world—and indeed give to the world that which God has so uniquely given him.

This is what happens in the most complete degree when one of God's children finds his true relation with his Elder Brother, his Master, and Lord and Savior, Jesus Christ. That love relation sets him free to live and love in the world. Indeed, most of us will not be able to be whole people, and give ourselves wholly in a marriage relationship, until we have first discovered our true selves by entering into the fulfilling love relationship in Christ which God intends for us all.

It's like the father of the bride saying, "Losing a daughter? No! I'm gaining a son!" Personality and identity are not denied in marriage. They are fulfilled and given a chance to flourish in marriage. If it is entered into in love! If it has faith at its heart. Admittedly, that is a big "if." People can destroy each other in marriage. They can use the marriage bed and the whole marriage relationship as a scene for working out their own frustrations on another human being—dominating, defeating, and even destroying him.

But that is not marriage's fault. That is not something commitment and the holy relationship of a lifetime do. That is something selfishness, and lovelessness, and demonic pride do.

What's beautiful is the shared life together God gives us with another person. That's why marriage is worth preparing for and preserving something sacred of oneself for—for bringing your best self to it.

With love, and with a pure promise to each other, with a baby—that is the most beautiful and joyful human relationship there is, and it makes for the growing of two people together so that in all the best ways they become one—one heart and mind, one purpose in life, as well as one flesh.

Have you ever noticed how much alike long-married couples look? Often that is the look of happily married people. Love does that! People in love for many years come to look like each other. Yet they are more truly individuals, because they have shared one life in heart and mind, and even in body.

Why shouldn't marriage be the beautiful sharing experience of fulfillment together that is happy beyond anything the independent, uncommitted life lived only for oneself could give?

Robert Louis Stevenson was a man fulfilled and deepened by his love and marriage. He wrote of his mate:

Trusty, dusky, vivid, true,
With eyes of gold, and bramble-dew.
Steel true, and blade straight
The Great Artificer made my mate.

Honor, anger, valor, fire,
A love that life could never tire,
Death quench or evil stir,
The Mighty Master gave to her.

Teacher, tender comrade, wife,
A fellow-farer true through life,
Heart-whole and soul-free,
The August Father gave to me.

And so He will give to you, and to the one you
love true, as you come to Him in marriage, with
lives pure, and good, and new.

8

And Then, There's the Need to Know Yourself

The big question among the long-haired young and the college crowd, is "Who am I?" A young college man whom I very much admire said once to me when I asked him how his life as a sophomore was going: "Well, this year I'm trying on different personalities for size."

That's what's so hard about being a teen-ager's parent: you have to stand by and watch him try those different personalities, which to you seem to fit not at all. You want to shout: "George, for heaven's sake, can't you see that that's not really who you are? You're being so fakey, and you don't even know it!"

But the search goes on, and it must go on, as kids seek the life style that will be right for them—the one they will want to live with for the rest of their lives. And they're really so great, these kids of today. They have such a sense of being a generation, of being part of a special group of people. Their long hair and baggy jeans are almost a vow of poverty, a struggling attempt to join the poor and the outcast of the world, to take the abuse of preju-dice for their long hair that the blacks take for the color of their skin, to see themselves as one in the spirit with the ghetto poor.

Their parents have lived by ideals of social accept-ability and corporate ambition. They have hungered for status and amassing of more and more "things"; while the kids hunger for something of the heart— some compassion, some caring about the lost people of the world. They've heard about the virtual slavery of the blacks of South Africa, and something inside them says it's wrong. They've seen the films on television of what their own country has done in war to a tiny agricultural people in Southeast Asia, and morally their stomachs are turned. They remember Martin Luther King, Jr., and how he was killed; and they sense something terribly wrong in the very soul of their own country, their own people, maybe their own home.

And they are very critical. All the institutions receive their scorn—corporation and state, university and church, home and country club. They are repulsed by their own suburban, often affluent, upbringing; and they want to have a new identity. They want to change it all.

They are very bright, too. They are top students. And their commitment to concern is such that they are not likely, no matter how long they live, to completely reverse themselves. They have made their judgment on society, and even when they move into it they are going to remain its critics.

All this is grounds for a deep morality, a fine sense of justice, and viable commitment to purpose. Concern and protest and righteous anger make for positive personality, for having a direction as one sets out in life.

And it is that purpose and sense of direction which is one of the great things a man and a woman ought to bring to marriage. People who get married ought, if at all possible, to be somebody before they take that step. Not that they shouldn't mature and become something finer together, as the years of marriage go on. But be somebody before you're married. Bring a real, live person to your marriage.

Many couples come to me for counseling before marriage, with apparently no star to guide them, no anchor to hold on to, and no sense of a hand they can hold on to for guidance and help. Too often they are without a sense of an overriding purpose for their lives or an honest sense of who they are.

Many of them haven't even that passion for social justice that burns within the hearts of many of their contemporaries. But the other side of their contemporaries' struggle for selfhood is their struggle, too—the fascination with drugs, dreams, and demonology, with alcohol and independence and sex, even as part of the search to find and understand themselves.

How, I ask myself, can you bring anything to another person in marriage, unless you have some sense already of who you are? And how can you be a person unless you are beginning to know who you are? So many of the kids I marry have little sense of great standards by which to judge, or any picture of love at which to look, or a sense of self to give them assurance.

That's why I feel sometimes like cartoonist Al Capp's Marryin' Sam—just getting people hitched for a price, without regard to whether they're right or ready for each other.

So I plead with those who contemplate marriage, particularly young people, to be a person, to make a sincere, dogged effort, as the Greeks say, to "know thyself." Know who you are, what you stand for, and what you care about. Because the day comes all too soon in marriage when the courtship excitement is over, and the round of parties and presents leading up to the marriage is over, and you've got to get down to work. It will be time to do a job, to be someone in a community, to have some kind of influence outside your home, and indeed, to have some influence inside your home other than being a great lover, or having fun in bed.

Which is not really being facetious. I am convinced that for many young couples the biggest thing they have going for them is their sexual attraction to each other. Their courtship is built on a lot of increasingly high-powered necking and petting. My question is, What do you do after you're beyond being fulfilled just by hand-holding, and kissing, and indeed going to bed together?

One finds after a while that there are many hours left in the day: that there is a job to do—maybe two, if both are working. There are relationships with neighbors to establish, and a relationship with the whole community. Who are you going to be in that community? What do you want your collective influence to be on the social, economic, governmental life of the city where you'll be living? Will you be in the PTA, the League of Women Voters, will you coach Little League boys, will you be a part of the church? Will you try to make a difference? Will you work for reform in local government? Will you try to improve the local library? Will you be a couple whom the community will begin to recognize as people of value, people who care, people who do things and change things?

And besides, you owe something to each other. There are books to be read, great music to be heard, issues to discuss, ideas to explore. "Man shall not live by bread alone," nor does he live by sex alone! He has a mind, a heart, a spirit. And the plea is— bring a mind and a heart and a spirit to the girl of your dreams and this man after your own heart.

The other person in your marriage deserves something more than an immature schoolchild who pouts when his own way is not gotten, who drinks when faced with problems and decisions, and who becomes angry and resentful at news that a baby has been conceived.

Of course, you can't hurry up growing, and what you get if people are going to be married at twenty to twenty-five is someone who is twenty to twenty-five. You don't get the maturity of a forty- or fifty-year-old.

But could not young people who plan to be married deliberately ask themselves some of the basic questions of maturity, of life, of issues, just to see where they stand and how much they know? And then together, try to grow? This process would even take a little emphasis off the sexual thing, even though it is directly related to marriage and their future. It could even be a little exciting to read some books together, to talk philosophy and life together. And why not try going to church together, and thinking about what God is saying in the Bible and in the church's message in preaching? Maybe Christ's compassion for the poor, His love of humanity, and His caring about little people would strike a responsive chord in young people whose generation has said it already shares these concerns.

The testing ground in the realm of morality as to who you really are will always come during adolescence. It comes in the form of the question: What will you have in your life—cigarettes, marijuana, LSD, alcohol, sex with anybody (as long as you have a good "relationship")?

The Book of Proverbs says: "My son, if sinners entice thee, consent thou not." Enticing sinners, of whatever stripe, be they "the boys" with whom one goes out for a beer or the evil companions of the Prodigal, are a test of a person's integrity. It is a test of our wholeness and the confidence which allows us to make the choice. When we're tempted to do things inconsistent with our character, it is because we don't understand our own character. We are not quite sure of who we are. We try drugs, because we don't know enough about ourselves to understand that we do not need drugs. We play with sex outside of, or before, marriage, because we haven't faced the fact of how deeply opposed our inner personality is to it. We do stupid, immature things because we haven't yet found the answer to "Who am I?"

Other people may know the answer: they may look at our insistent, driving course toward some unworthy goal as if a classic Greek tragedy was opening up before their eyes. They cry out, seeing clearly as day the disastrous fate awaiting us; but we go blindly on. Often, because they are the best friend, or the teacher, or parent, or sometimes the husband or wife, who knows us best (better than we wish), our pride dictates that we ignore them.

We think we know ourselves; and yet, for most of us, it is only on a far distant day that we really come to have eyes to see. It takes oftentimes "a heap o' livin,' " or at least a lot of trying, a lot of seeking, a lot of growing. A frustrated mother said to me once about her teen-age daughter who resists the counsels of her family: "I just know that someday she'll say, 'Mother, why didn't you make me shape up, and go to the right college, and stay away from a boy who wasn't good for me!' " We are so bull-headed, sometimes, when we are young —all because we don't yet know who we are.

Standing over drinks at a charity ball once, a rather self-important young newspaper man tried to impress me with how well he had caught the essential spirit of Jesus—particularly His nonconforming, nonchurchy spirit. He insisted: "Jesus was the kind of guy who would care enough about me to go out and get drunk with me in order to show He loved me and wanted to save me."

He was wrong. The Jesus I know would go to the ends of the earth with any man, particularly that young man. But He wins us on His terms, not our terms. He doesn't have to go over to the devil's side to prove anything to us. And certainly not to prove how tolerant He is. He doesn't have to get drunk, or play around with women, or steal, or lie. He is His own man, and He remains true to Himself. He comes, out of love, to help us discover our own true selves, and through Him, to become better than our best. He certainly doesn't come doing those things we were already doing!

Most of us are rather different people at forty than we were at twenty. Believe it or not, we've only just begun to see ourselves and accept the fact that we are who we are, and that we are not, and may never be, some of those things we had once dreamed of being. We've finally decided to live with who we are. That it has taken so long is not particularly to our credit. But that it finally happened at all is at least a sign of great hope.

Many of us look back over twenty years of marriage and see that it's only by a miracle we have survived all that growing and all that changing. Which may not seem very hopeful if you're twenty and want to be married right now—even to the person you know is the one for you!

Life is a bundle of risks, and marriage is one of

the greatest of those risks. But it's a risk to be taken, and taken gladly. But let faith be at the heart of the relationship, and let it be at the heart of your own life. And in that faith, you and your girl or guy, take a good long look at each other, and face the fact that you're going to change, and should change. That you'll both be developing as persons, and that you are persons now, already. And together, try humbly and prayerfully, and openly and bravely, to discover what you have to offer each other not only in physical love, but also in intellectual stimulation, in comradeship, in basic values and high principles. Then you can each say gladly, to the other, "I am I, and I at least have a sense in my heart of who you are. And I rejoice in what you are, for that is what I seek and long to have added to my life, in companionship and encouragement. But I am also glad to be me, and I believe I can offer you a true self, an honest person, to be your friend, and your companion, and your lover, all the way! Through all the years, friend, even to the very end. 'I know who I am, and I know who's going with me!' "

When you know that, you have hold of something far more important than the wedding license, and all the social trimmings. You're ready to give it a try. Go then, and be married, and God bless you!

9

Having the Grace to Learn from Others

The Book of Proverbs says: "My son, hear the instruction of thy father, and forsake not the law of thy mother: For they shall be an ornament of grace unto thy head, and chains about thy neck."

When you're young and in love and wanting to be married, you're often still in that stage of thinking that parents really don't know much. You think of all adults as old-fashioned, prudish, and just out of it in terms of all you know about the new, modern world you're living in.

The idea that parents could know something about love and marriage worth passing on has hardly occurred to you. Parents have been seen in the role of their responsibility for their kids so long that the latter have ceased to view them as real people—as lovers for instance, or as lonely individuals, struggling to keep their heads above water in this crazy world.

I remember so well when, as a Harvard sophomore, my Radcliffe freshman girlfriend and I had arranged a meeting between our two sets of parents. We knew we were awfully young, but we knew equally that we were in love and were going to be married someday. I'm ashamed to think of it now, as I look back, for my concern was not what impression I might make on my future in-laws, but rather whether my pious parents would make

73

a proper impression on my girl friend's parents.

It was disgraceful, as I recall now, what little confidence I had in my parents to do or say anything right. Actually I needn't have worried. They survived very well; and surprisingly, we all survived very well that day. It was something of a revelation to me.

Teen-aged young people would never admit it, but they are among the most prejudiced people in the world. They see others in categories and preconceived patterns almost more than anybody. And they surely are prejudiced against parents. It is through the eyes of prejudice that their parents seem so obtuse, so stupid, so un-with-it.

So, to overcome that prejudice, to outgrow that narrow view of other people, especially older people, and most especially parents, is truly a sign of a certain grace, the beginning of a little humility, the growth of maturity. A maturity, incidentally, which will be desperately needed in their own marriage. Kids leap into marriage and parenthood almost before they have outgrown their own prejudiced views concerning parents.

It's scary—that in-between time. It happens almost too fast for the transition to take place. But it's a nice thing if it can take place before the young couple is married—not only so that the parents can enjoy those few months or years of humility in their kids and enjoy being accepted by them, but also so that the kids can grow in their humility before they launch off into their marriage.

Grace and humility are so "key" for any life. And the grace and humility to learn from other people is so key in preparing for one's own married life. Because it again unlocks and opens up the way for young people to become more truly themselves, to become persons in their own right, before they are thrust into the responsibilities of marriage. To come to a marriage as persons already opening into maturity puts you so much further ahead than if you enter marriage with even that basic adolescent growing up yet to be accomplished.

So this chapter is just a little plea for willingness to learn from others. To say, "Well, maybe I don't know everything there is to know. How did you find it in life? How was it when you were our age? How is it at your age now? Can you tell us anything you've learned about the marriage thing that we ought to know?"

Given half a chance, there are people around with a great wealth of experience to share about life—especially life together. Like about the things that make you happy and the things that make you sad. Like about the things that bug you about another person and how you work them out. And, in fact, a lot of things about love.

There's a place, for instance, for listening to your parents. There are some things they have learned about life. Why not, for instance, learn from other people's mistakes? What can you lose by listening? In a day when youth holds the world by the tail, it might not be a bad balance to listen to the elderly, to respect the mature, to lend an ear to parents.

One of the greatest privileges I have is to regularly visit old people. I have learned to love them very much, also to respect them. A very bright spot for me once was to sit by the bedside of a lady on her eighty-ninth birthday and give her communion, hearing her confess with honest tears streaming down her face: "I need to be forgiven. I don't want to have anger and hate in my heart. I'm not that kind of person.'' She was old enough to be my grandmother and to have kept her weakness and need to herself. But she was also old enough to admit her need, and to learn, and grow, and change.

Sometimes older people, even middle-aged people, are mature enough to have grown beyond the necessities for one-upmanship: for having to be right, for knowing everything that's worth knowing, which afflicts so many of us, especially the young. Sometimes what older people have learned about marriage is that it's a long, hard struggle, and that they've done some stupid things that they've regretted ever since. And sometimes they've learned that they don't lose as much face as they used to think they would, if honestly and ingenuously they admit the mistakes they've made. Sometimes they've learned that ''confession is good for the soul.''

Like—they might tell you, if you give them a chance, about the mistakes they made, about the ways they hurt each other, and about what they learned, through pain and anger, over the longer years of married life. Can you imagine that they too might have married young—maybe too young? That they hurt each other with their little selfishnesses? That they ever were angry and sullen, too hurt to talk to each other for hours or days? That even they, your parents, had times when they didn't understand each other and hated each other?

Can you believe that, with all of their being respectable citizens, believers, and all that, they had their struggles too, like the rest of the world? That they had their time of unfaithfulness, and loving another who was not their own? And that they, in their young middle life had to look at themselves all over again, see the sin of their souls, and confess their sin and acknowledge their pride, and to say, in tears, "I am so sorry. Forgive me please, and let me try again to live with you and be true to the promises I once had made, and now have broken." Can you believe that even they, your outwardly normal, pedantic parents, were suffering the tortures of the damned, while you looked on, and did not understand? Can you believe that they were forty before they learned that they could not live unless they lived by faith, that they could not go on unless Jesus and His love came into their hearts in a new and deeper way, and bought them back from death, and saved them through faith to a new life of prayer, and sharing, and holding hands, and appreciating each other, and finding joy all over again? Can you understand that the Bible became their Book because it was the only Word that pointed them toward hope out of despair, toward light out of darkness, and toward life out of death?

They might even tell you of their courting struggles with sex, and how they, even they, had to fight the good fight to preserve that bit of chastity that they wanted to give to each other at their marriage.

They might tell you, if you pressed them, about money, and how you deal with it, and save it, and learn not to be burdened and broken by it. They might tell you about stewardship, about giving away to those in need what they needed for themselves.

They might tell you about arguments, and how you can live with differences. And about irritating little habits, like leaving clothes around in the bedroom, and not closing drawers, and rolling up the toothpaste tube in different ways. They might tell about the stupidity of self-righteousness and about learning to be accommodating.

If they have humility enough to confess their sins and share their sorrows and show their hopes to you, maybe you can have humility enough to listen and learn from these you'd grown to think had nothing to tell you that you didn't already know. The "ornament of grace upon your head" which the Bible says will be ours if we listen to our elders' instruction is the spirit of humility which is cast about those who become secure enough in their own personalities to be learners.

I commend it to you. It's part of real life and you could learn from your parents. It may even save you a bit of agony on your own at a later day.

Nobody, after all, likes a blowhard. The arrogant know-it-all is an insufferable bore, and the world casts about for ways to extricate itself from his presence. But the world is drawn to the humble person. He doesn't have to ask for the world's honor or hearing. The world comes to him freely, lending its ear and giving its honor, because it knows that this person is humble enough to care about all people. That he's been around enough, and been hurt enough, and humbled enough, to know that all men have something to say, all men deserve a hearing, all men have something to give. That's why he's willing to learn from the world.

You, too. You, too, be a listener. Listen to what love has learned—and you'll bring a far wiser and a far better person to your marriage.

10

Knowing God and Letting Him Know You

I know it's all very well to say, "Be humble. Be a listener. Get grace in your life!" Nobody would argue that it's a good thing to do. But how, man, how? How do you speed up that maturing process that brings you enough security so you can admit you're wrong, and really want to learn from somebody else? People don't find humility overnight!

Frankly, I have no answer to that but "God." I don't happen to believe people can just make up their minds to be humble. I don't think it's a natural virture, nor is it easily achieved. I'm not sure that any human being, given his sinful and proud nature, is capable of becoming humble at all on his own.

Humility, I think we'd have to say, is sort of a gift. It's something you receive, not something you manufacture or create, Grace is the freely given gift. And it's given by God. And I have to admit that I have nothing to sell in all this marriage thing but God. He's the one who makes the good marriages, and who rescues the bad ones.

So if you want to be a tolerable sort of person as you enter your marriage; if you want to have balance, and understanding, and maturity, and grace, and humility, and kindness; then get it from God! He has it to give and He wants to give it. Which will take some willingness on your part to give Him a try. Try letting Him into your life.

Which is truly getting to know Him personally.

When life is all over, and in its last dying moments you see it whole, there won't be any question about the importance of God. You won't have to be convinced of His significance for your life. It will be very obvious. But it will be too late. It won't do you any good then. The time that God can do you some good is now—right now!

The Bible says, "The fear of the Lord is the beginning of knowledge, but fools despise wisdom and instruction"; and that pretty well states the problem. Real knowledge, true understanding, intellectual integrity, education itself, if you will, begins when you have a healthy respect, a "fear," of the Lord. When you take the Lord into account as part of the scheme of reality, as part of the process of the world, when you give Him the place in your thinking that He deserves as the Lord of all and as the key to the universe, then you're on the way to knowing the things worth knowing, toward being a balanced person.

When you have a sense of awe and humility before God, you're beginning to know something. You're beginning to get smart. Because then you are beginning to understand that you're a man, that you don't know everything, that you don't control your life, that you're just a little bitty part of a great plan: one member, one little tiny child, in a huge family. To put it in Biblical terms, you are beginning to understand that you are a sinner. That you have needs. That you are not self-sufficient. That you're one of those "people who needs people"—and who even more than that needs God.

People who contemplate marriage without a personal God in their lives, I believe, are courting catastrophe. Because failure in marriage is a product of pride. It's always someone's vanity that's been touched by the attentions of a lover outside of marriage. So he starts thinking he has really "outgrown" his partner. There is the buildup of wounded pride that two people feel from the insults they've hurled at each other and the cutting remarks they've made. All through the drama of marital difficulties, in one way or another pride becomes the wedge driving two people apart. It's pride that's become the "fly in the ointment"; pride that is the nemesis, the stumbling block.

And the only antidote to pride is penitence before God. Get down on your knees, expose yourself to both God and your partner, and say, "Lord Jesus, I've made a mess of this; and I'm sorry."

If you don't take God with you into your marriage, who will redeem you when love runs out? Most young people just getting married are shocked at the suggestion that the day might come when they in fact would not love each other. "Who, us, not love each other? That's crazy! We're for always—for keeps!"

So they say. But the statistics belie their confidence. What arrogance gives them the right to think they could never be that one married couple out of every three on the American scene who are destined for divorce—who literally cease to love each other?

I see couples very often—beautiful people who have all kinds of good things going for them—who say bold-faced, "I just don't love him [or her] anymore." I've witnessed a man turning directly to his wife and saying those devastating words: "I don't feel anything for you anymore." And I believe it. Signs of real hatred were there. I've come to believe married love can be killed: can be suffocated to death, or beaten to death, or frozen to death, but in any case caused to die.

If that's true in your situation, but you don't want your love to die, where do you go? If you want to fan it into a flame, giving it a chance to grow warm and bright again, to whom do you go—to a marriage counselor, a psychologist, a minister? Maybe to all three; but not one of them can give you back love, once it's lost. Who has it to give? Who can salvage the sinking ship of your marriage when you're too hurt and angry to even talk to each other?

Same guy as always. The Bible's hero. God. More particularly, Jesus of Nazareth in whom God came into the world bringing His love. He passed that love around, sharing it with everybody, even the hard-hearted and closed-minded, for whom He died on the cross—"while they were still sinners"—so they could see, in spite of their blindness, how loving He was.

He's the only one who has it to give. All the rest of us have to get it from somewhere else. Only He is the source, the spring that bubbles up constantly with love. "Ho, everyone that thirsteth, come ye to the waters, and he that hath no money; come ye, buy and eat . . . ." "I am the water of life. He that drinketh of the water I shall give him shall never thirst again."

"God is love," the Bible says. That means He's the one where it all comes from. He's the central supply of love, of laughter, of gentleness, of beauty. When He made us, He gave us a supply of love, a potentiality for immeasurable love. He blessed us again with love when He married us. And if, in the meantime, we have squandered that love, by perhaps hoarding it for ourselves and refusing to continue giving it away to those we had promised to love, then we have to go back to Him for more. There is no other way.

And if you think that's all just a Christian fairy tale, and that you really don't have to go berserk over the Bible or go nuts over God in order to get your love back, then try it another way. I have never seen a couple able to wish love back, or rationalize themselves again into love.

The heart is not an instrument of logic and reason. It does not do the expected thing, the natural thing, or necessarily the correct thing. It operates by intangible instinct. It is spirit. And it moves by spiritual laws. And I have never seen a husband and wife at the brink of divorce turn back from their course because they had been presented with some logical, irrefutable argument by family or friends, or lawyer or minister. Not even by the argument that "the children will be hurt" (as they always are), or that "you've invested too much, economically, emotionally, and in time and effort into your life together to break it up now."

Those arguments never appeal. They do not succeed. People "out of love" are very stubborn, very hurt, very angry. What they lack, and what they want, is love. Often they've already got their eye on someone else who they think can give them love. But even that turns out often and again to be a will-o'-the-wisp.

Eventually, as a last-ditch thing, after they've tried everything else, people turn to God. They give Christ a chance. And He gives them what they've been looking for. He gives them love.

Often I hear it pointed out how many loving people there are who do not believe in God, supposedly proving that one can have love without God. A doctor friend of mine has had the same experience with that kind of argument. "I've examined and have come to know many people who have no God," he observes. "Some of them appear kind and generous. But underneath, I have discovered that they are often selfish, unbending, and without compassion. Wherever you find real love, there you will always find God." That's my experience, too.

Get to know God. Do it together, as husband and wife. Go to the places where He is talked about. Get to know people who know Him. Keep your ears open and your eyes peeled. Try to catch the signals of what the God thing is all about. I think you will discover that the God thing is a person—a loving, ever present person who cares about you, who has good things to say to you and marvelous ways to help you.

If you give Him an opening into your life you will find Him real and tangible—"an ever present help in time of need." If you let the Bible be your book, and the church your place of listening, and prayer your means of conversation, you will find your relationship with God deepening your relationship with your husband or wife. In praying together and honestly asking God's help in breaking down the barriers between you, the walls will crumble and communication with the one you once loved will begin to open up again. You'll be given grace to say you're sorry. In fact, you'll be able to say many things in your common prayer to God that you had been afraid or too proud to say to your husband or wife. The secrets, the hurts, the hopes will come out while you're on your knees praying. And they will begin to be dealt with there. God will deal with them. He will forgive them and heal them. He will open your hearts so you can talk about them. In beginning to know Him you will begin to know each other.

And you will discover that you are known. That the Lord Jesus knows your name—very well, in fact. That He knows your history: "all my trials, Lord." You will see that He has known you as long as you've been alive, and indeed, even before you were born. He knows your pet peeves, the little cuts that have hurt you, your early fears, your later worries. He knows all you've ever done, or thought, or said.

And, miracle of miracles, He still loves you! Even knowing your worst, He loves you! How's that for a friend? You don't often get that in your human relationships, do you?

Do you remember the little scene in John's Gospel when Nathanael demands of Jesus, "How do you know what I am like?" And how Jesus says, "Oh, Nathanael, I saw you a long time ago, under the fig tree. I know all about you!" That was quite a revelation for Nathanael: to see that he was known. That Jesus really had known him all along.

At first it was scary, wasn't it, Nathanael, to have someone else know those things about you that you always thought you'd take to your grave as a secret. But then it became a beautiful thing. A release. A relief. A setting free. Because Nathanael was known, and at the same time loved! He didn't have to hide any more. He could be himself. He could hold up his head. He was accepted. In fact, that's when he knew that Jesus was for real. "Sir, you are the Messiah!" He just broke loose in faith and life.

Our early married love was a little like that, too. It made us feel free and whole and loved. We wanted to sing and shout.

The struggle in most of our lives is to be known that way, to have that kind of friend. To have someone understand and accept us. God, in Christ, is the only one who ever will completely know us. And He always has. We have no secrets from Him. Never did—even though we may have thought so. He is also the only one who completely accepts us and loves us. He gave His life to prove it. That's why the cross is a crown of hope. That's why those who choose the cross and its Christ are the ones who are ready to love.

That's why, if you and your husband or wife are ready for Christ, you will find to your joy and happy surprise, that you are ready for each other. Ready to really know each other, and to be known, all the way.

11

Keep the Love-Light Burning

Love is such a precious thing. But it is also such a fragile thing. How easily it can be hurt. How deep can be its wounds. And how quickly its hurt can turn to hate.

That's the way it is with love. So much is at stake. So little does it take to blot out its light, and bring on the night. The poet says:

> The mind has a thousand eyes,
> And the heart but one;
> Yet the light of a whole life dies
> When love is done.

This is the single biggest problem in the marriage business: keeping people loving each other.

You don't need to be a cynic about marriage to recognize that getting along with one other person, in close quarters, for fifty years—particularly if you throw in a few kids along the way—is a monumental challenge. The best of the much-publicized new communes of six or eight sophisticated, free-living, un-hung-up, unshockable young people are reporting an average life span of not more than one to two years. And they started out thinking they could beat marriage all hollow!

Marriage is a fantastic endurance test. All the demands that can be put on the human spirit are put on partners in marriage. Just getting along, being nice, trying to consider the other person first, goes against so much that is selfish in the nature of man. After all, you're stuck with this other person for life! No matter how great a person you think this guy is, no matter how many good qualities he has, no matter how much you love him—indeed, no matter how true and deep a faith you share with him—before you have lived very many years with him you will have found a whole string of faults. Those annoying idiosyncrasies are part of who he is. Some things he can do something about, and some he can't or won't. And even to talk with him about those faults may become increasingly difficult to do—just because the mention of them wounds him so!

All of which doesn't mean you're sorry you married him. It means that just the sheer day in, day out making it together is a huge challenge to the human spirit, and will demand all you have: all your best psychology, all your best love, and all your deepest faith.

It's a lot to ask. A great deal to expect. And yet, despite the poor track record marriage is having in America, people are still lining up to get into it. Young girls still dream about their wedding day, and young men still hope there'll be somebody out there who'll care enough to have them in marriage. Even those who consider themselves so free and untrammeled by human relationships that they have adopted the life style of the sleepers-around with only "now" as their consideration: even these eventually seek the stability and permanence of a love with one special person, in marriage.

The record is still the same in America, and gradually growing worse. And many of us see every day the crushed remains of the lives no longer lived. We see husbands and wives who once dreamed love's dream together, made a life and even added years—till it all turned to tears.

Not that they did not love at the beginning. They looked at each other just as Elizabeth Barrett once looked at Robert Browning and asked: "How do I love thee . . .? I love thee with the breath, smiles, tears, of all my life!"

Most of us have said that, back at the beginning. And yet, how many tears have come. How many cutting, cruel deeds we've done—without ever really meaning to. But they've left their mark.

So how do you keep the love-light burning in marriage? How do you live and stick with it long enough, as the Book of Proverbs says, "to rejoice with the wife of your youth" when you are old? How do you keep love alive, and its fire warm, and its light bright?

At least be wise about the facts of love. Don't be naive. Don't let yourself be kidded into something. But don't become cynical by the model of marriage you've seen among the worst examples in American life—even those sometimes offered in your own home or neighborhood. And don't be duped by the expectations that advertising or films or novels would raise.

Ask around. Listen to those who are married. Learn the balanced truth, which, in the end, is the wonderful truth. The truth that, in spite of its agony, it also has ecstasy, and is still worth doing.

But be wise. Gain a little wisdom. Go in with your eyes open. Marrying is one of the two or three most important things you will ever do—second only to taking Jesus Christ into your life. And it's not worth doing on impulse or because all your friends are doing it and you happen to have an available guy. It's not even worth doing because the alternative of being a proverbial "old maid" seems so much worse.

There is always time, in most young lives, to wait a little longer, and be a little surer. There is always time to see how well the gal or guy you love endures if he or she has to wait. There are many couples whom I wish I'd cautioned to hold off, give it a year, gain a little more understanding of each other, be a little more able to strengthen and encourage and truly love each other.

Do what the Book of Proverbs says: be wise. "My son, attend unto my wisdom." And interestingly enough, Proverbs becomes very specific about love and marriage and false starts in love. It talks about discretion, about temptation, and about loyalty. It talks very realistically about the continuing temptations in marriage. About adultery. About "the lips of a strange woman" and how they are sweet as a "honeycomb"—but how her "end is bitter as wormwood." It says you'd better "ponder the path of life," because its ways are movable, and you cannot know them. Face the facts of love!

Proverbs tells it the way it is. It says: "Love, friend, is a strange business. It can lead you astray. You'd better know what it's really about." There's a sharp young generation of liberated cosmopolitans who nevertheless are making some serious mistakes in marriage. Do you know what you're getting into when you play around with love?

One of the movies to follow the early success of *The Graduate* makes a game of love: a wild, silly, early morning summer vacation bedroom game of unmarried sexual love. And the city boy and the country club girl carry on their game in her parents' home for weeks, through a long blissful summer. Presumably they love each other. The boy begins to feel the girl belongs to him. But the shocker comes on a weekend in the fall, at her college, when his summer bedtime companion suddenly does a turn-about. She lets him know that, all things con-sidered—like their difference in family background, social status, and the kind of future she really wants—he is unfortunately an inconvenience. That is, he's had it. And he walks away from the hotel where he'd arranged to meet her, into the rainy night, with sagging shoulders, a sad but wiser boy.

Too bad! He didn't know that love isn't something you play with. It isn't something you can keep, with-out commitment. Sex in itself doesn't hold you to the heart.

Did you know how wayward the human heart is, and how fast it can change its mind? That, in fact, it is capable of loving many another life? And that capacity and temptation to love another do not necessarily cease when you marry someone. The fact is, you could love another. The heart looks over many a high wall—if you let it.

So the problem of staying in love isn't a matter of the first night, or the honeymoon. Any fool can fumble through those first few weeks! But how about when a baby is on the way, and you, young man, are sexually sent to outer Siberia for a month, or two, or three. It gets very cold out there. Very lonely.

Especially after it was so great just before the baby came. No menstrual periods to get in the way, and your wife seemed suddenly so free—perhaps even freed-up—in her giving of herself sexually. She was beautiful—just the way they say pregnant women are beautiful. She knew that she had con-ceived a child, and that that instinctive female worry could be done with.

And so all those seven or eight months had been a veritable second honeymoon. But now this—this isolation while the baby comes. This taking second place as your mother-in-law comes barreling in to get in on all the action, and all eyes turn toward the new little stranger who's come to your house. And you're supposed to be the most ecstatic of all.

Intellectually, you know you are still just as loved as before; but you don't feel very loved! You feel left out. You feel cheated and slighted.

How do you deal with that? How do you keep the love-light burning? Well, you keep trying. You hang in there and manage to do some of the cooking and dish-washing—and maybe more. You may even get in on the baby-changing detail and learn how to hold your nose with one hand and swish the little things around in the toilet bowl with the other. By the time the next six or eight weeks have passed, you're feeling rather virtuous.

And finally, one night, you mumble something to your wife like, "Here I am, dear, remember me? Old George, and I love you still. Would you love me?" And when she looks up from breast-feeding (with its own sexual as well as deep psychological satisfactions) new little George, Jr., and reacts with surprise with, "Why, George, how could you think of sex at a time like this? Here I am, doing my thing with my baby—bone of my bone and flesh of my flesh—and all you can think of is sex! You beast, George!" What do you do then?

If you had not thought it through months before, and reminded yourselves that this is the way it would be, and had planned some reactions beforehand, to assure each other of your love, you are very likely to make some cruel remark and storm away, leaving your bride hurt and angry.

And just as probably, all sorts of wild things go through your head, like, "I'll show her! She can't do this to me!" And you storm out the house, maybe seeking out an old girl friend or looking up an old buddy. You're looking for ways to heal your wounds and assuage your hurt, and most of all to get back at that unfeeling woman whom you thought loved you so much.

And this only begins to suggest some of the angry, tearful things she's thinking about you!

Hopefully, before you blow it, maturity and love come to the rescue; and you're delivered from doing any one of those stupid things. But you've been hurt. And it's one of those first big crisis times for a young couple when they need all the savvy and understanding and tenderness they can muster.

And they'll survive that time if they've been wise—if they've sat down, long before, and taken off their rose-colored glasses long enough to see that married life will have some frustrations and misunderstandings. It doesn't mean that they have to blow apart over them; but they can talk it out and make some compromises, giving more than they feel like giving, and taking less than they want to take. Then they'll survive that time and be stronger to face the next.

Having a baby, naturally, is not the only crisis a couple faces. And the psycho-dynamics of that experience are not all bad. There is so much of joy, with the possibility of deeper unity and more bonded love. There are job crises, and identity crises, and success crises. There are also forty-year-old crises.

And all of them will be weathered if trouble is taken, very early, to build a basis for tenderness, for "hanging tough" and being true, for seeing that love can be entirely durable, lasting, eternal.

There is, after all, more to love than sex. There is more to marriage than a boy and a girl. There is more to life than growing old. There's something called being true, forgiving, and starting new. Something God can give to keep the love-light burning. Be wise enough to see that this is your need, too.

12

Be Friends with Each Other

Another key to keeping that love-light burning is to make sure you both stay friends. That you don't let enmity cross your threshold and curse your household. That you stay "pals forever." That you keep on liking each other, having fun together, sharing yourselves the way real friends do.

Remember what Proverbs says? "Let thy fountain be blessed; and rejoice with the wife of thy youth." Not only, as in the last chapter, "rejoice with the *wife of thy youth*"—with the same girl you married when you were young, but "*rejoice* with the wife of thy youth." Don't just doggedly hang onto the relationship, don't just spin it out into years, but let your relationship continue to be enjoyable to you both.

Be happy with her, and satisfied in her love. Don't be always looking for something better, some gal who appears to have more to offer than you think she has. "Let her," the Bible says, "be as the loving hind, and pleasant roe." That takes a picture from nature: a gentle, spirited deer, with a capacity for affection and a growing relationship.

It's interesting that the Bible says, "Let her be as the loving hind." Let her be tender, let her be beautiful, let her be supportive. It's worth acknowledging that in many human relationships one person frequently does not allow the other person to be loving, to be gentle—sometimes to be even interested; maybe even civil! Some people have a way of bringing out the worst in other people. They are so adept at baiting them, or criticizing them, or just grating on them, that they are rendered incapable of responding with warmth. All avenues of face-saving have been cut off and all opportunities to reach out in gentle support have been denied. They have barricaded all approaches to themselves, so that is becomes impossible to have a relationship of kindness and gentleness with them.

Constant badgering of a husband or wife by the other can so turn down the heat in a marriage that after a while there is no love left. "You always hurt the one you love," the song sings; and most of us have learned through experience that you sure do!

A friend of mine freely admits that he himself killed off something precious in his marriage which ended in divorce. He was a swinging ad man in the radio-television industry, and there were a lot of parties to go to. He drank just enough on those occasions to bring out some of the hostilities he felt for his wife. By his own admission, he ridiculed her and cut her down in front of respected colleagues and their wives, until she hurt so much that when the opportunity came she filed for divorce and the breech was never healed.

"Let her be. . . ," the Bible says. Let her be what she can be. Let her fulfill herself. Let her find the personal destiny to which she is entitled.

A lot of men are afraid of that. A great challenge is flung down to their masculinity when a wife pleads the right to "be herself." Lots of us are threatened, wondering: "Does that mean she isn't satisfied with me, and with our life together? Does she think she

96

has more talent than I? Is she unhappy at home? Am I inadequate?"

Oh—wow! We can think of all kinds of things —which usually aren't the point. Usually, what she wants is not some women's liberation revolution in her home life, but a more subtle freedom to do some of the things she loves, and to have a regard shown for her that recognizes the uniqueness of her spirit. Which, in the end, might even make her far more interesting and more fun for her husband.

Maybe she is subtly forced to play a role—to be part of her husband's professional or business role—so that she isn't free to be the most exciting, interesting self that she can be. In most cases, if she was given this freedom, it would make her not only more appealing to her husband, but more useful to his career. It would be a better role than the one he mistakenly puts her in.

And "letting her be" can also apply to being beautiful, too. I wonder sometimes if many married women are not kept from being beautiful by their husbands. Not that their husbands say: "Dear, you work too hard at looking sexy, and wearing nice clothes and getting your hair done, and your face fixed up, and your stockings always right and your nails always clean. I could care less!" On the contrary, most of us are too often carping at our wives to go to the beauty parlor more often, and wear sexier clothes, and be more fetching. We're all for it!

But maybe being told that they ought to shape up isn't what makes women beautiful. Maybe being loved, and supported, and served as though they're loved is what inspires them into beauty. If beauty isn't skin-deep, then it evidently has to well up from the spirit inside. Maybe it comes from being gently dealt with, and appreciated, and encouraged. "Let her be," the Bible very wisely says.

And it's also saying let her body always be beautiful and attractive to you. Let her companionship, her counterpoint of character, her laughter, her intellectual zest, and her capacity for compassion be a maturing thing. Let it be better than ever at forty—and fifty, and sixty—right on until it crosses over into heaven and the most beautiful relation ever!

Some of that's going to have to be self-discipline. It's going to have to be what the eye sees: the proverbial vision in "the eye of the beholder." What constitutes reality is not only an interesting philosophical question; it is a vital, practical question, especially in marriage.

It is possible to see what one wants to see. It is possible to see intangible, spiritual things—things that are very real, but which are not often captured in the sex-accented eye of the studio camera, nor seen in the voluptuous models who drape today's advertisements. The movie queens and the females who get on television are a powerful force in blinding us American men to the real beauty of our own wives!

Consider. Wrinkles around the tummy are a disaster for any 24-year-old lithe model whose career depends on firm breast, long lash, and taut tummy. But maybe there's something beautiful, even in wrinkles, if they come from the carrying of a child. And if her breasts at thirty-five or forty-five are not so firm as those of the model in her twenties, perhaps they have a special beauty because they gave milk, and life, and incidentally love and understanding to little babies who now are beautiful people in this world of possibilities. And if crinkles around the eyes come on a mother who's smiled a lot and forgiven a lot (remember?), perhaps there is beauty there that no luscious secretary or model can ever match.

But to be able to see that, young husband, and particularly not-so-young-husband, that is the test. Not so much the test of your imagination, or your vision, as of your character!

And the principle goes for all the other things beyond physical beauty: character, intellect, and laughter, too. They have their ways of being seen and felt. Why shouldn't a wife and mother (yes, and now a grandmother!) be a thousand times more interesting to her husband and to everyone around her, than the cute young chick who might more quickly catch her husband's roving eye? Old men are often found "appreciating" young women. And that's okay. But how much more important that they have eyes of love and hearts of understanding to appreciate what is truly beautiful in this gorgeous woman of depth and spirit who has been their companion of a lifetime.

And men, after all, often do not have that much to commend them against the same standards of measurement. What business does a 45-year-old man, bald of head, pink and full of cheek, flabby of muscle, and expansive of girth, have in being interested in a young woman half his age, who has a beautiful body? What qualifies him? Surely, not simply that he is a man! And what qualifies him to expect anything of his wife in physical beauty if he has done nothing to have it himself!

These are questions of fair play, and, hopefully, of putting the whole matter of love (and its basis in friendship) on a deeper and more appropriate level.

It kills me to think how far from this ideal most marriages are. To think how unappreciative and unsupportive so many of them have become. One man confessed to me, concerning his wife of thirty years, "No—I really don't know what she thinks. We don't communicate much anymore." And that could be multiplied by hundreds and thousands all across our land. I sat with another man once at breakfast in a motel restaurant. He hailed a friend and business associate, and explained later to me: "Oh, he's living here. His wife's in an apartment, and he's here."

For some of us, whose job is listening, the problems pour in. Problems of defeated people who feel trapped in a relationship that's become something they never had expected nor would have deliberately created, but which they have ceased to care to change. They're in it, they don't seem to be able to alter it, and far too many of them see throwing in the towel as the only answer.

The previous chapter's movie of misled young love also painted a picture of misled middle-aged nonlove that was even more devastating. It recorded the late-night bedroom of the girl's middle-aged parents, revealing the taken-for-granted, unexciting matter-of-factness familiar to far too many twenty-five-year marriages.

The father pads sleepily about in his shorty P.J.'s, finally laying himself down in rumpled disarray on the nuptial bed to pluck a few more grapes from the bunch he is holding, philosophizing vacuously about young love to his grim, determined wife, who sits bolt upright on her side of the bed, seething about her daughter's romance with the unacceptable young man from the city. All the while she's staring at TV from under her swathed hairdo, massaging her middle-aged hands with lotion and carefully covering them with little white gloves to preserve their waning beauty.

Natural enough it would be to say: "Who wants marriage if that's what it's like?" That is certainly part of the reason why some of the young think they can do better without marriage. But it doesn't have to be like that. And Proverbs is saying that beautiful marriage is possible. That love, and laughter, and life together are possible, if you can learn to be friends along the way. If you can learn that the other, too, has a life to live, and a contribution to give. That the other has something to say as you walk life's way.

Friends are people who stay in touch, who have hearts that share, who somehow see life through similar eyes—and find their relation a continuous surprise.

It is pride that is the enemy of that kind of friendship in marriage. It is pride that dims the love-light, and pulls us apart from each other. It is the kind of pride that pushes toward success, toward the name in lights or on the letterhead, toward the position of power. It is the pride that causes those lonely nights at home for the one he loves—which become lonely while we ambitious men are so busy succeeding. In the meantime, our wives are left to seething, or to just doing their suburban housewife "thing," until, at the pinnacle of our ambition, our whole world we were so busy trying to create has proved to be a house of cards that comes collapsing down from within. And with it, all that we had worked for crumbles into dust.

All because we—perhaps both husband and wife—were moving too fast, and that way missed love's thing that had been waiting there, in the long years of married life. The tragedy, as Francis Thompson says, is that

> 'Tis ye, 'Tis your estranged faces,
> That miss the many-splendored thing!

Don't miss it, young lovers—or old lovers. Be friends along the way of love!

13

Make Faith Your Foundation

I am so tired of having beautiful young couples from church families come to me without any faith. They all assume it's natural that they don't believe anymore. They are not ashamed. They do not hang their heads and say, "I'm kind of embarrassed to be coming to you to ask you to marry us, because I've decided I can't live up to the pledge I made to Jesus at the commitment service, when I was fifteen. I haven't been keeping the covenant with Christ and with the family of our church for several years now. I know it's pretty inconsistent to be accusing the church of hypocrisy and irrelevance—and still want to be married in church."

No, for the most part they don't make any confession like that. They come, sometimes, feeling a little bored at the idea of having to spend two sessions with the minister as a sort of requirement for getting married in the church of their choice. No matter that they grew up in this church and perhaps were once in the confirmation and youth program of the church. They're really not part of the church anymore, so their "family" church becomes the "church of their choice." The church building of their choice. It's still a pretty place to be married, even if they don't believe what the church is all about.

I wonder why some of them hadn't gone to a

justice of the peace to get married. It would be all perfectly legal in the eyes of the state, and there wouldn't be any of those religious strings attached. But still they come, bold-faced, and expecting to be accommodated.

And they are. I'm a sucker for kids. Especially bright college kids who used to be Christians. Because I'm praying like crazy, and bidding like crazy in my sessions with them, for a new faith, a reborn belief in Jesus as Lord and Savior over their very personal lives.

Sometimes I know I miss, and the bride-to-be, who once was a little girl in my class, goes away in tears. A few times they've said, "O.K., if that's the way it is; then we won't be married in this church." In the meantime, naturally, they condemn us as stodgy, self-righteous, and unbending. Because they do not understand what we are all about. One has the feeling that they think the church is there to do their bidding—to marry anyone who asks. And by the same token, to baptize or bury anyone. The idea that the church has principles is inconceivable to them. That the church thinks it makes a difference what you believe, that it's in the business of something called Christian marriage, not just any kind of marriage—that's a whole new idea to many of today's young couples.

But I do accommodate. I take them where they are, and try to lead them along, in two or three meetings, to understand some things they didn't understand before. I try to show them the straw man they've constructed in their view of the church so they could feel comfortable in rejecting it. I try to point out their prejudices. I try to open them up to Jesus and to the church. I say, "At least agree to being pilgrims together. Be willing to become seekers after God. Don't pretend something you aren't; but be honest about your unfaith, and open your life to finding faith. Be willing to give Christ a chance in the new life you'll be building together.'' That's my plea. All I ask is that they be honest enough to be open.

And most of them are. Most of them were not that comfortable with their rejection of faith. There is something in them that would like to believe. Something that recognizes that perhaps they've been unfair. For some, not much changes. For others, a new life begins; and their marriage becomes truly a Christian marriage.

I press the faith on these young couples because I am an ambassador for Christ, called to take every opportunity to represent Him and to deliver His message of love, asking for their answer of commitment. But I press it also because I believe that without faith, marriage doesn't have a chance. That without God's love in a marriage relationship, the deepest and truest love, which He gives, doesn't have a chance. And frankly, that without God the marriage itself, no matter who the couple are, has the cards stacked against it.

The key to marriage is having faith as the foundation of love, having something eternal at the heart of two lives. The world thinks, ''Ah, love! man, that's what makes this thing beautiful. We'll live on love!''

I've sat with scores who thought they could. But they're not married now. It all broke up—in one shattering disaster of dismay. Because the love-light died. For lots of reasons. Like getting out of touch, and waking up one day and finding that it's not the same. The bright and shining light that warmed your life is suddenly cold and dark, and you find yourself concluding that you'd just as soon get out.

What holds two people together when that love-light has died? What keeps a marriage going when you think everything's been tried? Faith, my friends. Faith in the forgiving, healing Jesus, Lord over that home.

If you're people who think Christ has been near through every midnight tear, every secret fear, you'll turn to Him—even when you cannot turn to each other. You can get down on your knees together and say:

> Here a little child I stand
> Lifting up my either hand;
> Cold as paddocks though they be,
> Here I lift them up to thee."

It doesn't take anymore than that: a silent request that Christ come close. And He mends the tear. He "knits up the raveled sleeve of care." He binds the wounds. He bridges the gap. He does all that, and more—if you love Him and ask for His help. And mean it.

One of the most deeply touching experiences of my life was to stand before two parents, after they had been separated for two years, and hear them say their vows again in the presence of their little children. They'd been hurt and broken, but finally they wanted to try again. But only after they had formally pledged themselves all over again in church, would they begin living with each other again. They wrote new and beautiful vows, and said them directly, unrehearsed, to each other—looking the other in the eyes and meaning every word of what they said. And that pledge they made not just to each other, but to God as well. They wanted Him to be part of their marriage this time. Done so very simply, so very lovingly, so very faithfully, so very genuinely, and therefore so very hopefully.

I believe anyone can do that. But it's work. It's embarrassment. It's confession. It's saying, "I'm wrong and I'm sorry." It's saying, "Jesus, I really mean it now: I want You. I need You, and at last I'm ready to do what is necessary to get You into my life!"

Any couple can resolve to live the life of faith, to lay foundations in belief that will last their lifetime together. And they don't have to wait until they've been married ten years and realize their marriage is in trouble before turning to faith as a rescue mission. They can start right off.

They can simply say, "We believe that here is something good that we can program into the computer of our minds and hearts to be there to help us, as stored information, as active influence during the years of our life." They can, in fact, go so far as to say, "Well, in our teens and early twenties we programmed enough stuff into our lives that was bad that we'd just like to give God a chance now. We certainly gave alcohol a chance at us in those fraternity parties. And we gave marijuana and speed a chance to give us some kicks on an experimental basis. And we certainly fed our minds with a lot of sex stimuli in movies with bedroom scenes. And what with smoking pretty regularly, and being of a generation that uses foul language without even thinking of it anymore, we've let rather a lot of pretty garbagey stuff have quite an influence in our thinking. And we sure haven't gone to church very much in these years. We figure it's about time God had His inning in our life. Especially now, when in a sense, we're starting all over again, beginning a new life. We want it to be the best life it can be. We want it to be happy and to last, and we hear faith can help. So we're not ashamed to give it a try.''

Getting married, after all, is serious business. Why shouldn't young people make a considered decision about what they want in their marriage? They've certainly spent time talking about the question of children—how many, and how they want to raise them. They've talked about friends, and style of life, and work, and what part of the country to live in. They've talked about sex, and birth control, and common interests, and all that. Why not talk about Him who is the heart of the universe? Him to whom every human life is ultimately related? Him who has proved to be the longest lasting influence for good in human history for the last two thousand years? Why not deliberately choose to have in your life the greatest influence that anybody, anywhere, has ever heard about?

And it's never too late, either, for long-marrieds to make this kind of decision. To say, ''Perhaps we've got only twenty years left—or one year. If Jesus is a good influence, and we don't have Him in our marriage the way we'd like, let's start now! So we did boot it with our kids, and never taught them much about Jesus. So we've lived our lives without Christ for a long time, and have developed a style of life which doesn't look as if it really fits with Him. So our friends will think we're nutty and may reject us. So we will feel we must ask for ginger ale or tomato juice at cocktail parties and wedding receptions. It's worth it! We'll do it!''

Do what? Suddenly be ''religious''? Well, maybe. It may seem that way, at first. But basically, become disciples. That means ''learners.'' Jesus' disciples were with Him to learn. So, as disciples, they lived a disciplined life of following Jesus. They tried to walk where He walked, often struggling to keep up with Him. They tried to listen to what He said, and to get the point if they could. They tried to keep their eyes open to what He did, and the effect it had. They learned by watching. What they learned was love, and faith, and prayer and perseverance. They learned to go much further in the things of faith than they'd ever dreamed possible. They saw prayer working miracles. They saw love changing lives. They began to understand the supernatural: that God was in the world in their friend and teacher, Jesus. And that He could be in the world in them.

They became new men. Jesus loved them into a whole new style of life. Could we do that in our marriages—walk close with Christ, imitate Him, begin to key into His power, begin to love with His heart?

Our discipleship could start by finding a church that we dig—one that "speaks to our condition," as the Quakers used to say. It would be a church that is a company of Christians who seem to have Christ in their midst, and a love in their spirit, and a message in their proclamation.

We could make up our minds that meeting with these people and being confronted by their Lord at least once every week is something we're going to do, if at all possible. When the church bell rings, we're going to be there. And with sufficient rest and readiness so that it won't be just in body. Saturday night will always take into account Sunday morning. That's going to be prime time for learning, for inspiration, for healing and reconciliation, and for meeting and making Christian friends.

So there's a start, albeit a formal, traditional one on the surface. Even that decision may take a little guts, though, when you think of the cabin in the country, and ski week-ends, and fall hunting, and all the rest. Discipline it will be, indeed.

What else is it? Knowing Jesus. Listening to Him. Learning about His life, His love, His will, His teaching, His commands, His call—to us. Can we get hold of something to read, to study maybe? Yes. It's called the Bible. Try *Good News for Modern Man* or *The Living Bible* (a paraphrase).

Read it. Alone? Sure. For a few minutes—maybe even a half hour a day. But read it together also. Like at the breakfast table. Or if that's too frantic with rushing off to work, try reading it after the evening meal. You'll miss sometimes, maybe many times; but try. Doing it together is priceless. Husband and wife. And then children. Read a little and then pray. Or talk about it first, sharing your thoughts about it. Ask what it says to you as a family.

And let everyone get in on the praying. The most beautiful prayers will be the children's. Don't miss this in your own lives!

Prayer is communication. That's our conversation with God through Jesus, our friend and interpreter. That's when we can talk with Him, and He with us. Make prayer a "must" in the new discipline. Pray alone, in the morning. Even if it's just a waking "Oh, thank You, God, for this new day!" And look, don't ever have a meal together without a prayer. A thanking prayer: for food and being together. And pray along with the Bible reading at night. And finally, when it's time for sleep, take hands across the bed and share a prayer. And when, out of that bed and its love, little children have come, stand by their beds at night, and lay a gentle hand on their heads, and pray for them and with them—for God's keeping of their lives. If you begin early with such a practice, they'll never want it otherwise.

But act out your faith with others, too. Find some place where you can serve, by meeting a human need, in Jesus' name. Volunteer in a hospital, teach an inner city child, care about your neighbor in his time of grief, teach a church school class, serve on a committee, go to the troubled. Be a minister!

Find friends with whom you can meet intimately once a week or once a month, to report on your pilgrim's progress, to share faith and love, and maybe read the Bible and pray.

Start here, in these simple things. They will lead to much more. To whole new relationships and ultimately to a very new life. And the marriage undertaken or renewed in this way will be a very different kind of marriage. A far more living marriage, because its foundation is faith.

14

Don't Be Too Cynical to Trust

Nearly twenty years ago, as a young parish minister, it became my privilege to visit frequently an elderly man in his nineties. He was a remarkable gentleman. He had been a parish minister most of his adult life. He was the scion of a clan of three generations of parish ministers in the Presbyterian denomination who were famed throughout their fellowship. The "grand old man" himself had been hugely successful and widely known and loved throughout many years as a pastor in Youngstown, Ohio.

One day at his hospital bedside we talked about the great tradition he had been part of, and of some of his significant accomplishments in this ministry. And then he said something which, to me, as an ambitious, starry-eyed young minister, seemed hard to believe. He said: "You know, in spite of my love for the ministry and my joy in many successes and happy associations through it, my deepest satisfaction in life, the thing I am most proud about, is to have been the father of four fine sons. It has been most gratifying to have given them a start, and seen them succeed, and do likewise with their sons and daughters. This is by far my greatest accomplishment in life."

My first thought was "How quaint. How surprising for a successful man to put the raising of kids above everything else." Now that I am older, with kids of my own, I can understand. It is a major task to get kids through childhood, and through their education, and to help them understand themselves and get out there into the world of adulthood and responsibility.

And for most of us, one way or another, sooner or later, that's what it's about. Simple, naive, old-fashioned, unglamorous as it may seem, that is one of life's greatest tests—raising your kids and getting them through.

And yet the whole relationship between parents and children is, in any generation but particularly now, one of the most tense battlefields of human life. Surely it is one of the most crucial tests of marriage and family life. How do you do your thing with your kids? How do you listen to them, and encourage them, and prepare them?

Who are you to think you are going to be able to build bridges across the generation gap? And who are you to think that your own marriage will sail through all the challenges that children raise to its success? How are you going to give hope to your youngsters and at the same time have hope for yourselves and your generation?

Is it too naive to suggest that the key is trust? I would like to suggest that trust is a key to both marriage and to the family relationship with children that grows out of marriage. And my plea is that you won't be too cynical or too sophisticated to let trust be a factor in your life.

And trust is a lot to ask these days. A brilliant, critical generation of young people have symbolized their cynicism about the adult "straight" world—its values and loyalties—in a widely accepted philosophical assumption that you "don't trust anyone over thirty."

This generation, wearing its hair long and its clothes bell-bottomed in symbol of its rebellion, has thumbed its nose at what have seemed to them the commitment to materialism and self-preservation, and even dishonesty, of its parents' generation. Even in the matter of faith, they feel that their families have not been sincere. It seems to them that their parents have been committed to doing not what was best for the world, but for themselves.

So they haven't trusted their parents, or a lot of other people. They have tended to be cynical of anyone who espoused high ideals or religious principles. Chastity has become something you tolerate or even laugh at, rather than look to as an ideal for your own premarital life. You suspect anyone's motives if they are idealistic and selfless.

This means that many human relations are looked on in different ways than they once were. It means a woman can achieve the front page of a national news magazine as a person who is "liberated" in every way, as one known to have had "meaningful relationships" (presumably including sex) with a number of well-known men without ever having been trapped in marriage, and be viewed almost universally as an ideal for a whole generation of young people.

Which is not to say that nobody wants to be married anymore. But it is to say that even those seeking marriage often philosophically see nothing wrong with free sexual relationships without formal marriage. They choose marriage, but they admire that one who gives it alone with a series of men in what she calls "little marriages." And the reason they accept it for her, and are not shocked by it, is that they have come to see love (along with much else in modern life) as something you can't trust. To invest your whole self in it is to be sort of a fool.

Which is why they love Kahlil Gibran's advice to be like "the pillars of the temple" and not stand "too close together." For themselves they want marriage. But should the present situation ever change, should their love fail and fade, why, the thing to do would be to get out.

In many ways they do not trust anyone. The world is "plastic." Everyone's a fraud. Everybody's got some angle. The fact that they do not see their own fraudiness and their self-deception is merely the powerful testimony to how very human they really are. And someday, presumably beyond age thirty, they will see their own phoniness and self-righteousness. Hopefully, they will then gain a more mature balance, with a little graceful humility.

But the mistrust—often among surprisingly young people—goes on. It floors me when ninth graders guffaw or give cat-calls when some human plight or aching need is described to them; when high school students discuss cheating in exams with the shrug that "oh, everyone does it"; or when collegians say the same about sexual relations before marriage—as if that's just one of those things you do today.

So sadly cynical so many young people are. All of us have it to some degree, but it's painful to see it so widespread among the young. The simple souls, the trusting types, are so rare. Try to find one whose view of the world is a naive acceptance of all its beauty and truth as a kind of gift:

I believe for every drop of rain that falls,
a flower grows.
I believe that somewhere in the darkest night
a candle glows.
I believe for everyone who goes astray,
someone will come to show the way.
I believe above the storm, a smallest prayer
will still be heard.
I believe that Someone in the great somewhere
hears ev'ry word.
Every time I hear a new-born baby cry, or
touch a leaf, or see the sky, then
I know why I believe.

So simple, and so beautiful. So different from the spirit of pessimism, and suspicion, and hostility in so many human relations. But a hard thing for the young to achieve.

And yet the Christian faith has tried to nurture and teach that to its young people from the beginning. The apostle Paul wrote to his young friend Timothy: "You know they are true, for you know that you can trust those of us who have taught you."

And how might today's parents of teen-agers say, "Oh, Paul, silly boy! How far do you expect to get with that kind of a line. The very fact that they were taught it has become their most powerful reason for rejecting it. And to accept it just because they know they can trust us who have taught them—why, that's ridiculous. They don't believe that."

And of course Paul plods on: "You know how, when you were a small child, you were taught the Holy Scriptures; it is these that make you wise to accept God's salvation by trusting in Christ Jesus."

Now, this may be the point where suddenly Paul's argument could make a lot of sense. This could be the point at which our natural cynicism and failure to trust others, and even to trust our husbands and wives as well as our parents, could be broken down.

Because, of course, we haven't really expected our young people to be much other than cynics anyway. We expect them to rebel. Even in matters of faith we say, "Oh, that's natural for young Christians to reject their faith for awhile."

We've let it be natural, but was it accepted as natural in the New Testament church for young Christians to deny their faith and turn their back on their Lord for a few years? It happened occasionally. But it was the cause of agony, and tears, and remorse. It caused young Peter to hang his head in shame and say, "Depart from me, Lord, for I am a sinful man!" It caused Judas, in dismay and despair, to rush out and hang himself. It was not taken as the "natural thing." If you had publicly agreed to follow Jesus, it was assumed that was your stand for life. Devotion was expected of you. Perseverance. Faithfulness!

And yet we mouth such foolishness as that which I've heard from more than one young couple who say of their newborn baby: "Oh, we're not going to teach her anything about religion. She can decide for herself when she's of age." Pure cynicism. "Faith," they're saying, "the God thing, is too naive. Let the kids figure it out and choose what they want when they're twenty-one." But of course nobody does that with any other kind of education. Nobody waits around till their children are twenty-one, if it's mathematics, or English, or history that they want them to know. They would be idiots if they did, and their children would be completely unprepared for the intellectual realities of modern life.

And maybe they'll be just as ill equipped to deal

with the psychological and spiritual realities of modern life if learning about God is denied them, if a sense of faith and humility—even about the unseen world—is not given them.

But the apostle Paul says to young Timothy: "Keep on believing the things you have been taught. You know they are true, for you know that you can trust those of us who have taught you."

Imagine! He was saying, "This is not kid's stuff. It is true even though it is something you were taught as a child. Just as true today, Timothy, as it ever was. And you know you can believe it on the basis of your trust in those of us who taught you."

How about that for an interesting appeal? We're the ones who love you, he was saying. I, your minister, and your mother and grandmother, Lois and Eunice. We, of all people, would not kid you or lead you astray. You can trust us.

And that's just what would bring hoots of derisive laughter today. Your minister? Your grandmother? Your mother? Get with it, man! Those are the people most out of it. You know they're living in another world.

But what if these simple, naive things that get taught to children at their "mother's knee" are really the most profound things of life? What if children are really the wisest people, and what if their willingness to trust and believe is really the most important attitude for humans to have, and the one way they learn the most about life and ultimately become most successful?

What's significant is that Paul doesn't say, "Timothy, anything I say goes, or anything your parents and grandparents say goes—it's all gospel truth." What he does is point Timothy to something quite objective, quite beyond the mere opinions his parents, grandparents, and minister may have had. He said, This is where you can judge the truth, where you can become wise about human relationships. The Scriptures will teach you. They are objective. They do not lie. "You know, Timothy," he says, "how, when you were a small child, you were taught the holy scriptures. It is these that make you wise to accept God's salvation by trusting in Christ Jesus."

The truth here is that one trust is built on another. Trust mother and father, trust minister and teacher, as they teach you the Holy Scriptures; for the Bible will give the wisdom needed to trust Christ and accept from Him God's power to save you in every human situation, every human need. Like—you'll even be able to trust Christ to help you save your marriage. To help you trust your wife or husband beyond what you can see now; beyond the love you feel now. He'll help you trust each other forever. He'll give you the kind of trust that can go beyond a series of timid, temporary "little marriages" that never make a life, and never make a family. He'll give you a trust in each other that dares to believe life's ups and downs can be dealt with; that failures in love can be overcome; that even dullness in marriage can be renewed. He'll give you a faith that anger, jealousy, everything can be met and defeated, and that life together can be beautiful.

And believe it or not, He can even give you the kind of mutual trust that will make you honest enough and secure enough and humble enough to be believable human beings to your children. His kind of trust can give you the give and take, the penitence, and the spirit of forgiveness that will encourage your growing children to see you as people who also are human beings. They will see you as people who know their limitations, and who have enough humility to admit when they are wrong and therefore are to be approached and trusted.

And none of that is very sophisticated. It doesn't seem very cosmopolitan. It is certainly not swinging. It is really very simple and childlike. But so profound. "Unless you become like little children—with their simple trust—Jesus said, you'll "never get into the kingdom of heaven."

Beware lest we keep ourselves from trusting other human beings by becoming cynics. And beware lest we train the minds of the little children God gives us to mold, especially to reject His whole basis for trust. Beware that we do not so sell ourselves to the critical faculties as the only avenue to intellectual respectability that we create impossible conflicts for ourselves, and an intellectual monster for our children. Dare to trust!

In the Russian novel *The First Circle*, the author says of the character representing Stalin:

Mistrust was Iosif Djngashvili's determining trait. Mistrust was his world-view.

He had not trusted his mother. And he had not trusted that God before Whom he had bowed his head to the stone floor for eleven years of his youth. Later, he did not trust his own party members, especially those who spoke well. He did not trust his fellow exiles; he did not trust the peasants to sow grain and reap harvest unless they were coerced and their work was regularly checked on. . . .He did not trust the members of the intelligentsia not to commit sabotage. He did not trust his soldiers and generals to fight without the threat of penalty from regiments and machine guns in the rear. He did not trust his intimates. He did not trust his wives and mistresses. He did not trust his children. And he always turned out to be right.

The cynicism of mistrust is ultimately demonic.
Only the trust of a little child saves.

> Last night my little boy confessed to me
> Some childish wrong,
> And kneeling at my knee,
> He prayed with tears—
> "Dear God, make me a man
> Like Daddy—wise and strong;
> I know You can."

> Then while he slept
> I knelt beside his bed,
> Confessed my sins,
> And prayed with low-bowed head.
> "O God, make me a child
> Like my child here—
> Pure, guileless,
> Trusting Thee with faith sincere."

The Bible teaches us to be trusting—in marriage
and in all human relationships.

15

...Nor Too Ashamed to Do Right

"Being good," and "doing right" still have a very pious sound in American parlance. A goody-goody is somebody nobody wants to be—somebody not only naive about reality, but so sheltered and sequestered by his parental environment that he cannot bear to see the awful truth in the life around him. He's a misfit from the word *go*.

And yet we say of Joe Doakes that "he's a good man." Which means, on the contrary, that he is a regular guy, somebody who is able to deal with reality without having to sell out to it. And our world, interestingly enough, respects that.

The difference is difficult to define. Suffice it that *goodness* is a dangerous word and a misleading idea, and one about which many people—particularly young ones—have mixed feelings. So it's hard to ask young people of our day to "do right," to try to make their individual and their married lives count for "good." They are, naturally, a bit suspicious.

And yet many of them are committed to right, as they understand it, as few generations before them have been. They want to do right by the outcasts of our society: the blacks, the poor, the alienated. And their suspicion of all calls to "righteousness" from those middle-aged representatives of what they see as society's "established institutions," is based on their experience of those establishmentarians' commitment—in their eyes—to a variety of forms of respectable violence.

But to righteousness (as they understand it) they are indeed open. To moral right (as their elders understand it), having usually to do with sexual morality but including also drugs and alcohol, they are certainly wary and defensive—but not, I believe, closed.

"So what do ya mean, friend, by 'doing right'?" they might challenge. "Explain yourself. Give us some reasons." And "reasons" are exactly what too many parents have gotten away without giving, for far too long.

Yet what most Christians want for their grown-up kids is the kind of commitment to "right" that was Jesus' commitment. Social justice, by all means. Standing up for the underdog—the tax-collector, the woman taken in adultery—of course. But the difficult personal righteousness too. The personal purity that becomes an example to others. Like Paul not drinking (or eating meat offered to idols) lest he cause his weaker brother to stumble. It's the spirit of personal denial that comes out of "Let him who would be my disciple deny himself, and take up his cross, and follow me," and also out of Jesus' last prayer for His disciples, "For their sakes I sanctify myself."

In other words, it is the kind of righteousness that cannot be misconstrued, the kind that cares more about other people than it does for itself, the kind that demands of itself just as much adherence to justice and freedom from prejudice as it does from others. It is the kind of righteousness that tries to be as free from self-righteousness as it can.

People who love Jesus and are struggling to follow Him would like to see their youngsters grow up as people who have the kind of instincts that would help them to do the loving thing, the humble, self-sacrificing thing, and the courageous thing. They are hurt most when they find their kids in any way to have been mean, unfair, or selfish. They are shocked when their kids have done something that rides roughshod over the feelings of others—which may be what really hurts them at their kids' drug abuse or sexual relations. It's where someone else's life, as well as their own, has been opened to risk. They would like their kids to be selfless—in the spirit, and style, and pure power of Jesus.

Faithful parents, along with Christian friends, and supremely Jesus as He is known in Scripture and prayer, is the kind of background that opens up the way for young people to sincerely want to *do right* in the best sense of those words.

Once any of us have overcome our hang-ups about piety and can take a straight look at life, saying, "Here, by the grace of God, is where I want to stand. Count me in on the side of goodness, and justice,"—then all kinds of sources open up and become available to us in that quest. And believe it or not, the greatest aid ever given to us is the Bible. "The whole Bible," Paul wrote to young Timothy, "was given us by inspiration from God, and is useful to teach us what is true and to make us realize what is wrong in our life; it straightens us out, and helps us do what is right."

Facing what is wrong in our lives, of course, is almost more than most of us can bear. It is such a temptation to see evil in the world not only as purely social, but always having its root in someone else. We tend to see evils perpetrated on society only by bad people like absentee slum landlords, and uncaring capitalists, and brutal policemen, and insincere politicians, and selfish aging men in the power structure. It is very hard to face the fact that evil is in the hearts of all of us. "It is not that which a man takes into his mouth which corrupts a man," Jesus once said, "but that which proceeds from his own heart." It is their hearts that dream the infidelity, and prejudice, and cruelty which men seem ever capable of doing to other men.

And seeing that, honestly looking at it, takes a spirit of humility and a quality of confession that is hard for most of us to master. And yet the style among many young people—influenced by flower children and hippies—is a surprisingly confessional one. It is not built on an ability to always appear self-confident, but rather, it affects a tentativeness, almost an uncertainty, and with it an openness to new ideas and people, trying to be accepting of any who may come along.

It is considered among them very gauche to know what you are going to do in life, to have a profession all picked out, to have a long-range goal and purpose. The going style is to be unsure, to be short-range, to be almost convinced that there isn't going to be a long future—that one's life isn't going to last very long anyway. Truthfully, most of us, of any age, feel something of this uncertainty.

Our time as a whole has developed an almost confessional spirit—a desire to rip off the mask and to be our real selves—in the longing hope, I think, that someone would reach out a hand and understand.

And this spirit recognizes, if only unconsciously, that in fact there is something very wrong with man. That wherever you find him, he is covering up a whole lot of things—a veritable "can of worms" if you will—that really trouble him. He has a vague sense that just as "all is not right with the world," so it is also not all right with him. And he's really unhappy about that! He would like to do something about it.

Sometimes he thinks the psychiatrists will help him—and they do. Sometimes doctors, pills, and hospitals look hopeful; and they are. Vacations, sunshine, a new environment, even a better job and more money play their part and are not without value. But usually the last place he looks, the last option he seriously tries is faith: Jesus, and His church, and the Bible that recounts history and records His beautiful truth.

And yet the Bible is a mind reader in helping us see what is wrong with ourselves. It goes to the heart of the human problem—man's separation from God and therefore his separation from other men. The Bible calls that sin; the quality of having your back willfully turned toward God.

By humbly and faithfully and prayerfully reading the Bible, seeking to hear in it the Word God is trying to say to us through it, we can learn to know ourselves. And it can gently and wisely (sometimes dramatically) show us what a righteous life can be, what exciting and eternal values there are to live by, and what happy and humble forms of goodness there are. And not just for old-fashioned people, or for Biblical characters. But for cosmopolitan, sophisticated young people of today.

When the Bible talks about personal morality, for instance, it goes far deeper than the legalisms of religion against which the perceptive young have so often rebelled. It doesn't leave killing or adultery at just a matter of taking someone's life, or doing the act of sex. Jesus says if you're even angry with your brother and call him "Raca—thou fool" you're in danger of hell-fire. And He says it isn't enough to avoid outright adultery. He says, "If a man so much as looks at a woman to lust after her, he has committed adultery with her already in his heart."

Very subtle, the insights of Jesus' righteousness and morality! When you begin thinking this way it becomes a lot harder to be at the same time in favor of racial and social justice but also for free sex on a personal basis. To decry pollution and over-population with one voice, and with another to demand legal abortion and free day-care centers for illegitimate children conceived out of a view of sex that asked nothing of love or responsibility in a partner, is no longer so easy to justify.

To do right and to seek goodness in all human relationships isn't really too much to ask of young people. It's not too much to ask of a courtship or a marriage. Jesus is not afraid to ask it of any of us, of any age, who call ourselves Christians.

My plea for people contemplating marriage, and for those already married who are concerned about their own kids, is to say, "Give Jesus a chance. Let Him be your teacher and your kid's teacher. Let Him be your guide and example. Look at His life, listen to His teaching, hear the whole purpose of God for man in the heritage leading up to Jesus and on through Him into the New Testament church. Read the Bible, absorb it, and let your life be informed and formed by it.

There is something permanent that the Bible's expressions on goodness and justice can give our marriages. For people who work so hard to give their children so much of "things," it would be so easy to give them the gift of a great foundation in the spirit at so much smaller cost. We pour hundreds, even thousands, of dollars into our children's lives.

And yet the one thing that could do most for them, which could help them be happy adults, knowing right from wrong, we cannot be bothered with! A little prayer, a little Bible, weekly worship, and church school is the closest thing in society to a guarantee of doing right that there is. And it's here just for the asking!

It's that built-in guarantee God gives, that informs and guides, and troubles the Christian conscience. And once we have it, we can never get away from it. And ultimately, in our times of most terrible temptation and tragic need, it saves us.

In a book called *The Affair*, a psychological case study of adultery, it was this, in fact, that finally saved Neal Gorham and his marriage. This sensitive young man, happily married and the father of two children, had nevertheless fallen deeply in love with another woman he had met in a business way. He wanted a divorce, so that he could leave all and have his Mary. And yet, after long agony of conscience, he knew that he could not—that something deep within him, some ultimate and final commitment, would not let him go over that brink of family and personal destruction. He wrote in his diary:

> Last night Laurie and I had an argument till four in the morning, a stale rehash of every major disagreement of thirteen years. How can I be what I seem in her eyes, and also what I seem in Mary's? Too late I have discovered much about myself that I had not known. Too late because I have a daughter and a son who need me at home for another decade, a fading, too-plump wife who will probably not let go, and a Presbyterian conscience that will never give me peace!

As the apostle says, "The Bible is useful to teach

us what is true, and to make us realize what is wrong in our lives; it straightens us out, and helps us to do what is right." And not only can it give us an idea of what is right, and a desire to do right. It can help us be glad and to find joy in doing right. That is a great achievement for any person, or any married couple.

16
The Secret of Life Is Service

And finally this, my marriageable and marrying friends: the secret of life is service. The key to being happy, to fulfillment, to a sense of partnership with someone you love, is finding a life together in which you can do good for other people, a life in which you two serve the world.

Some of the happiest marriages I have ever known are those in which husband and wife were involved together in loving other people, helping them—in fact, sacrificing their own lives for them.

I think of a gifted young doctor, founder of an international medical mission serving in the mountains of South Vietnam, in the harbor of Hong Kong, in the desperately poor canyons of Tijuana, Mexico, in the backwoods hollows of Appalachia, and among the Navaho Indians of New Mexico. His wife, so inspired with his work, actually went to medical school—in spite of responsibilities for four growing children—in order to be a doctor and work alongside her husband. Tough time. Not easy. But happiness and fulfillment in that marriage!

I think of a husband and wife working with high school young people in conducting summer institutes on international relations. He a minister, she a Quaker, working for the American Friends Service Committee. And in those weeks with young people how many late, late nights endured, how many confused kids counseled, how many square dances danced, how many good laughs enjoyed, how many enduring friendships made. They became the anchor and the lighthouse to hundreds of young people. And dozens of hours they gave up when they might have been alone together. But happiness —joy in each other. Wow!

I think of a young headmaster of a New England boys school and his pretty wife. Living their whole life immersed in a tiny, isolated town in Vermont —far from cultural and intellectual interests and friends. But supremely happy giving their lives to boys. Receiving parents and students in their own gracious home, with the wife sharing as truly as her husband in the problems and potentialities of each member of their little academic family. A beautiful marriage, in service.

I think of another couple: he a college professor, she a teacher of nurses. No children, but a love of young people everywhere—their students, and their students' friends. Their interests are as wide as the world. They travel together to fascinating places on their school vacations. They take pictures. They introduce people. They make things happen. Now they're writing a book—together! Happy people. Fulfilled people. A marriage working.

I think of a still-young computer executive, with his own company, with his own varied financial interests, and his own time. His wife is a gifted artist. She and her daughter teach arts and crafts to ghetto children once a week. He chairs the board of directors of an international medical organization. They go to board meetings together and she helps put on an annual ball to raise money for the project. She believes in it and their two children do, too. As a whole family they work together, serving their brother man. And they find happiness in it all.

Add your own illustrations of these unusual and beautiful people. But why unusual? Everybody could be doing it, no matter what job the husband, or the couple, may do. All can serve. All can love people. All can give themselves away to help others.

The Bible, after all, is about loving other people and serving the world. It's a kind of ideal which all of us admire. "Do unto others as you would want them to do unto you!" "I was sick, and you visited me, I was in prison and you came unto me, naked and you clothed me." "As you did it unto one of the least of these my brothers, you did it unto me." "Those who have done good, shall rise to eternal life, and those who have done evil, to judgment." "He who loves God but hates his brother is a liar."

We'd all like to do good. Something inside us says we'd be happier if we worked harder at doing more good to others. Paul's letter to young Timothy says that trusting God and believing His Word to help us "is God's way of making us well prepared, and at every point fully equipped to do good."

"Well equipped to do good." Well equipped to be useful, to make a contribution, to help people. Of course we want that! And we want it for our kids as well as for ourselves.

Funny thing about that. Here we are, teaching our children to love their neighbor, and not to kill, and to turn the other cheek—and then we're flabbergasted when they grow up and begin doing just that! We teach them to "sell all that you have, give to the poor, and come, take up your cross and follow Christ"—and in their own way, they do it. They wear clothes from Ragsville. They identify with all the underprivileged and outcast. They want to be ghetto school teachers or social workers with the disadvantaged. They want to be volunteers in the black part of town or they want to spend a summer working on an Indian reservation. And we don't understand.

The Lord must be laughing up His sleeve at us parent-types who taught the Christian truth and the Christian way better than we knew. We gave a philosophy to our kids that we really weren't committed to ourselves.

And what a picture of us: paying thousands for the so-called advantages of life for our kids, when in our hearts we know that isn't what produces happy, whole people. Our affluent society is reeling with the tensions that come from the frenetic life of people who dart in a hundred directions at once in pursuit of that elusive goal of "success."

The secret we are so obtuse about learning is that happiness in any kind of life is a by-product. It's something that comes as a surprise, as grace, a free gift, when we are laboring in pursuit of something else. Happiness comes in the contest. It's part of the battle. It is in the striving.

And there is no more noble purpose in life than striving to serve others. "Greater love has no man than this," said Jesus, "than that a man lay down his life for his friend."

Husbands and wives who have no great goal in life, no dream that they share, have no compass point, no North Star, no real direction. They're just living life out, taking advantage of whatever may come along. They're not looking into the future, not seeing a vision, not giving up things together to reach the goal.

Frankly, they have time on their hands. They are cursed with a certain kind of "nowness" that lives without relation to eternity. But they have time to see too clearly what is lacking in their married life, what is defective in each other's personalities. They have time to be bogged down in those mundane and petty things that are part of all of our lives. They live small, and not great. They live narrow, and not wide. They live short, and not long. They live bound, and not free. They live selfish, and not giving. They live disappointed and frustrated, not fulfilled and happy.

Any person and any couple can care about others. Any family can serve the world. Any marriage can live by large dimensions. It's all in learning how. Actually in learning how to love—which is, ultimately, learning how to live. That's why Paul makes his point to Timothy about the Bible. "It is God's way," he said, "of making us well prepared at every point, fully equipped to do good to everyone."

So many beautiful people have already learned. One night in early fall my doorbell rang, and there stood a young college friend of mine, holding—hot from the oven—a "goosleberry pan dowdy" which he had picked and baked. It was a present, sort of a love-gift. Just out of the blue! But so typical of that boy. Canoeing with him the summer before and having occasion to wait at a portage for a ride out of the wilderness by motorboat, I had occasion to watch this lad cheerfully volunteering to carry up and down the portage-path the packs and outboard motors for other people. I don't know what he'll do in life. But I know this: he will do good!

Isn't there something in every couple's and family's life that can be committed to doing good, to loving the world, to sharing all it has? That surely is what the Christian life is all about: loving the world because Christ first loved us, gave us life, and taught us how to love.

Isn't that also what Christian family life is about? It's learning together to love, so that in its turn, the world itself, in all its need, may be loved.

> I listen to the agony of God—
> I who am fed,
> Who never yet went hungry for a day.
> I see the dead—
> The children starved for lack of bread—
> I see, and try to pray.
> I listen to the agony of God—
> But know full well
> That not until I share their bitter cry
> Earth's pain and hell—
> Can God within my spirit dwell
> To bring His kingdom nigh.

Florence Nightingale wrote:

> Life is no holiday game, nor is it a clever book, nor is it a school of instruction, nor a valley of tears, but it is a hard fight, a struggle, a wrestling with the Principle of Evil, hand to hand, foot to foot. Every inch of the way must be disputed. The night is given us to take breath, to pray, to drink deep at the fountain of power. The day, to use the strength which has been given us, to go forth to work with it till the evening.

What kind of weapons are we going to give our kids to fight with? What knowledge of the battle? And with what will we fight—life's whole battle, but especially the battle to love, and to keep on caring deeply and being Christian with this person we chose so long ago to live with forever?

Christians, we must not fool ourselves. We have nothing we can give our children, or use ourselves—no guarantee, no insurance—except the person of Jesus of Nazareth, God's great Son, who loves us with a passion and whom we can love with devotion.

There's a heritage for a new generation of young people. There's a foundation for love and for life. Nothing more is needed.

Still listening? That's what "Marryin' Sam" has to say. He could call this study *Married People I Have Known*, or *What I Have Learned About the Greatest Life There Is*. For what it is worth, through all the mistakes, through all the agonies, through all the darkness, and through all the triumph, I pass it on, with joy—and hope.

Let there be a new marriage in our land. A new loving, a new caring, a new daring. A new future.